EASY
PLANTS
FOR
DIFFICULT
PLACES

EASY PLANTS FOR DIFFICULT PLACES

in apartments, homes, and offices

JACK KRAMER

Drawings by Robert Johnson

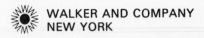
WALKER AND COMPANY
NEW YORK

First published
in the United States
of America in 1975 by the
Walker Publishing Company, Inc.

Published simultaneously in Canada
by Fitzhenry & Whiteside,
Limited, Toronto.

ISBN: 0–8027–0468–9

Library of Congress
Catalog Card Number: 74–82401

Printed in the United States
of America.

Book design by Barbara Bedick

10 9 8 7 6 5 4 3 2 1

Contents

Acknowledgements

During the course of this book I queried many friends about the plants they grew or wanted to grow in various situations—in their office if they worked all day, in small apartments or in homes where light was bad. These people deserve special thanks for answering my countless questions: Judy Smith, Eva Strock, James Carew, Genevieve Sussman, Robert Johnson.

Others, too, contributed unknowingly, when they called me to ask about a plant that wasn't doing well. Space doesn't allow me to list these first-aid calls, but they were numerous, and I appreciated the opportunity of getting a plant back on the road to well-being.

So to all people with plants and to all plants with people, I say thank you.

Introduction

When people see my garden room filled with thriving plants they nod their heads knowingly and say, "Of course, with ideal conditions like this anyone can grow beautiful plants." And they are right. It takes no great powers to have lovely indoor plants when light and humidity are optimum. However, there are also plants throughout the house (about sixty of them) in less fortunate places where light is extremely poor, where humidity is sorely lacking. Still, palms, ferns, philodendrons, cacti, and other plants grace tables, decorate corners, and bring cheer to the kitchen. These are the easy-to-grow plants that are really in difficult places.

I am no miracle worker. The reason the plants survive in these untoward conditions is that they are different ones from those in the garden room. These are the plants that survive if necessary with bad light and some neglect. The secret to growing these plants—if there is one—is proper selection of plants and proper care. I water and feed these plants differently than I do the garden room greenery. With less light, the plants assimilate food slowly so too much water or feeding will kill them.

Even if you have difficult places for indoor plants there are many easy ones that will make any brown thumb turn golden. And that is what this book is all about. Here we look at more than 200 plants—foliage and flowering ones too—that will grow indoors in almost impossible situations. And get ready for a surprise. Some of these plants are the most beautiful you could ever find.

—JACK KRAMER

1 Consider Your Plants

Quite frankly, your house plants are at your mercy; they depend upon you for all their needs. And they depend upon something else: the conditions you can give them. Before buying plants—and many look so lovely it's hard to resist impulse buying—consider that dark nook in the living room or that drafty place near the dining room window. If you know ahead of time what the conditions are and what kind of plants will tolerate these conditions before you buy, you'll have your plants with you a long time instead of for a brief visit.

When we buy furniture we know in advance where it will be at home; when buying clothes we know what weather conditions we are buying them for. Let the same rules apply to plants. Where will they go? What will the conditions be there? With plants as expensive as they are today it's wise to heed these rules. If you throw up your hands and say, "I don't have any suitable place for plants . . . it's too dark, too drafty . . ." think again. There are some plants that will accept these adverse surroundings and still add beauty to the home. True, they may not last years, but they will last a long time. In other words, don't give up before you start; know some of the following facts.

How They Grow

Contrary to most thought, in their native habitats most house plants grow where there is little, if any, sun, but they do grow in diffused or subdued light. Look at it this way: In the rain forest or jungle there are hundreds of leafy plants, nuge ones and not so huge ones. The biggies cover the little guys (the trees, that is), so a nice dark place nutures good growth. Philodendrons and anthuriums thrive in dark, moist places, as do ferns. Clivia, a beautiful flowering plant, thrives on the forest floor; it's obscured by giant vegetation yet still bears a bountiful crop of lovely orange flowers.

Many plants don't need or want glaring hot sun; it burns foliage and can dessicate a plant. So even if your apartment is dark, there's no excuse for not having green plants. However, don't expect miracles—only certain plants will do, which is what this book is all about. Bougainvilleas and other flowering plants—many of them—do need that sunlight. Don't be foolish and try for the impossible. Just be content with a fine philodendron and make believe it's a bougainvillea. It's easier this way than buying the flowering plant and having it succumb in a few weeks. So whether you have a purple thumb or a dumb thumb, forget it; I'll show you plants that can tolerate even a brown thumb.

Again, let me say that some plants do need and must have ample sunlight, but these house plants are the ones to leave to those folks with greenhouses and ample windows and ample time. The plants in this book are for apartments or homes where sunlight is often lacking, or for offices, for all-day green companionship.

Where They Are

Position is everything with plants. Just where you put them indoors will give the final yield: health or sickness. Sometimes just moving a plant a few inches one way or another does the trick. I found this out years ago; to this day there's a spot on top of a shelf in my kitchen where absolutely nothing—but nothing—will grow. Is it hexed? Are vibrations wrong? The explanation is simple: The air currents are bad there; the heat is stifling at that location.

So move plants around until they respond. Put them in one place, watch them for a week or so, and see the reaction. If the plant seems wan and limp, move it somewhere else until you find the right spot. You may cover miles in the first few weeks, but once settled, that's it, and you'll have saved miles of worry.

Specifically, if you have a dark corner, grow the following plants:

Aspidistra elatior (cast-iron plant)
Chlorophytum comosum (spider plant)
Cissus rhombifolia (grape ivy)
Dieffenbachia amoena (dumbcane)
Dracaena massangeana (cornplant)
Philodendron soderoi

If you have a drafty place with moderate light, try:

>*Asparagus sprengeri* (emerald fern)
>Echinocactus (many kinds)
>*Euphorbia splendens* (crown of thorns)
>*Guzmania lingulata* (star plant)
>Orchids (many kinds)
>*Pandanus veitchii* (corkscrew pine)
>*Plectranthus coleoides* (Swedish ivy)

What They Do and Don't Need

Here are some good common-sense hints about house plants:

The house-plant container holds very little soil compared with the amount of soil outdoor plants are in.

After the first two months there will be few nutrients in that soil, so weak feeding is necessary to replenish foods.

If light is bad, plants simply can't grow fast no matter how much water or food you give them. Water and feed sparsely.

If heat is high and uncomfortable for you, it will make it difficult for plants too; get some ventilation going. (A small fan works wonders.)

If your home is extremely dry and you have frequent colds or sinus trouble, so will your plants. Buy an inexpensive cold-water vaporizer to help you and your plants. (Don't buy a vaporizer that gives warm heat.)

Always be optimistic about your plants; think that they will grow. They have tremendous tenacity. Don't say they'll die before you start.

Forget all the foolishness you ever heard about balanced soils; this was fine years ago, but now packaged soils contain all necessary ingredients and take the guesswork out of mixing soils. Buy the packages.

These are the general hints. There's one more requisite a plant needs, but this I can't instill in you if you don't have it: namely, love. Or at least you've got to like your plants somewhat or they won't respond, even if you yell at them all day.

2 Natural Light and How It Affects Plants

To our eyes light is either bright or dark. But a plant sees things quite differently. To it, light is life, and varying degrees of light will affect different plants differently. Plants simply can't use nutrients without sufficient light, and plants in dark places will need less moisture than those in optimum light. This all seems simple until you consider the varying kinds of light, which directly affects other cultural routines such as watering, feeding, and humidity.

To further complicate matters, light in gardening books is classified in a multitude of terms, from bright light to scattered light, semishade, and so on. Some clarification of these "light" terms are necessary to intelligently cope with plants in their respective light sources. Also to be considered is that light changes as the seasons change and is less intense in winter than in summer.

A sunny place for plants indoors is an ideal place, but many apartments, homes, or offices may be sorely lacking in sun because of overcast days, buildings obscuring the sun, and what not. Bright light is more easily found; for bright places there are innumerable plants to grow. Many areas where you want plants indoors may be shady, but there are plants for this situation too. In each "light" area different plants will be used, and different ways of growing them are necessary. And that's what this chapter is all about: How to grow which plants in which locations and how.

Know Your Light

To most people shade indicates darkness, but this isn't so. A shady place would be the corner of a living room away from natural light sources. Semishade, a bad term to begin with (but used often in horticulture), means a place where it is mainly shady but with some natural light. Bright light has a gamut of meanings, ranging anywhere from bright to not so bright to some sun to little sun. For all practical purposes we define light as (1) *shady*—northern exposure, or away from windows, (2) *bright*—east or west windows, away, but not too far from glass, and (3) *sunny*—southern location (near glass).

The Shady Ones

We'll discuss plants for dark places first because most people have trouble coping with plants for these conditions. These plants may be in corners, along walls, or in rooms where there are few windows. It takes a special kind of plant to survive this situation and still add appeal to a room. Quite generally, these plants are naturally forest dwellers growing in humid, shady conditions, never in total darkness, and it's wise to remember this. (If your apartment is totally dark—a highly improbable situation in any extreme—then you must use artificial light for plants, as discussed in Chapter 11.)

Plants that will succeed best in shady areas include aglaonema, a leafy, richly colored foliage plant that never grows too large; aspidistra (cast-iron plant), a longtime shady favorite like the old-fashioned rubber tree *Ficus elastica;* sansevieria (and there are many), which can also tolerate trying situations; spathiphyllum, from the aroid family; and nephthytis, which will also grow in a less-than-ideal condition. Not to be forgotten are philodendrons, which can also adapt to varying conditions, and there are dozens in this group to beautify a room. However, most, if not all, these plants will never become too large or treelike (floor-plant size) but will remain medium-sized.

Ferns, however, will grow to a somewhat large size in shade (provided other conditions such as humidity and moisture are good). These plants include *Asplenium nidus,* the lovely bird's-nest fern; *Davallia bullata* or *D. mariesii,* both excellent lacy green plants, and ferns such as pteris, polystichum and polypodium. Palms, although generally wanting good light, can to some extent grow in shade too, at least the following ones have for me: *Chamaedorea erumpens,* the beautiful bamboo palm, and *Caryota mitis* (fishtail palm), an often overlooked plant. Ferns can be used with great advantage on pedestals for a lovely vertical note in the living room, and palms are always lovely room accents.

Ironically, cacti and other succulents, which we

think of as sun-loving plants, will also provide indoor beauty if you select some of the larger specimens from the cereus family. They'll survive for many years without too many problems on a sparse water diet and even in a dark corner.

Although I've mentioned quite a few plants for those difficult shady places, don't think that these plants will last for decades. They'll grow and be beautiful for a few years before they succumb to the trying conditions, at which time they should be replaced. But remember that a dozen roses for fifteen dollars last only a week!

Plants for Bright Places

Brightness means the average light conditions in an apartment or home where there are say, two or more windows. To further clarify, this means where lights *are not necessary during the day.* In this category there are dozens of good plants that will adapt to indoor conditions and continue to be handsome for years.

Immediately, splendid plants such as *Chlorophytum comosum* (the spider plant) and *Cissus antarctica* (kangaroo ivy) come to mind; these are lovely green accents without demanding much attention. Plants such as *Cordyline terminalis* (ti-plant) and many of the philodendrons are other good candidates for bright but not sunny places. *Pandanus veitchii* (corkscrew pine), an overlooked plant, also does well in only bright light. Small plants that never grow too large such as peperomias, marantas and pileas are also excellent for bright desks and tables or windowsills. In fact, with too much light these plants will perish.

Members of the bromeliad family (and there are many) can also be grown with success in bright places, and offbeat plants such as *Rhoeo discolor* (Moses-in-a-boat), *Kalanchoe tomentosa* (panda plant), and *Pleomele reflexa* are other fine subjects for bright locations. In addition, of course, any of the plants listed in the previous section can also be grown; indeed quite a galaxy of plants.

The Sun Lovers

These plants, and they include many flowering gems, need at least a few hours of sun close to windows to prosper and like shady plants, which require different cultural conditions from those in bright light, the sun lovers need buckets of water and excellent humidity and additional feeding to grow well.

For those people who are fortunate and have some sun amidst the darkness there is joy in store for you. There are some lovely plants to bring color to rooms and *Clerodendrum thomsoniae* (glory bower) tops the list. This is a large plant with dark green leaves and dramatic red-and-white flowers. *Dipladenia amoena* (Mexican love vine) is very popular and in sun bears handsome funnel-shaped shell-pink flowers. If ginger is your dish (to grow that is), try *Hedychium coronarium,* a medium-sized plant with shiny green foliage and white blooms. Without a common name but lovely is *Heliconia aurantiaca* with flowers that resemble (to me, at least) the bird-of-paradise. Impatiens, the dwarf garden kind, is still another fine indoor flowering plant that offers a bounty of red flowers, and an old favorite, *Abutilon hybridum,* called flowering maple, with bell-shaped orange flowers, is always desirable.

There are, of course, many other indoor plants for sunny places, but this is a book about plants for difficult locations so I have only mentioned the above. However, if your heart is set on flowering plants and you have very little sun, *there are still plants for you.* They are in Chapter 7, and there are quite a few lovely species ranging from orchids to gesneriads and so forth. Something for everyone.

3 Don't Kill Them with Kindness

Plant people are generally kind; they love their plants, but all too often they give them too much attention. This can cause problems with plants growing in dim areas. Don't smother your plants with a constant marathon of water, feeding and warmth. You have to be sort of a meanie to keep house plants in dark corners alive because they simply can't take too much water or massive injections of fertilizers. But this doesn't mean total abandonment; simply use some common sense.

Watering plants has been a mystery for indoor gardeners for years, and even though there are no universal rules, there are some simple answers. Feeding too can present problems, so we'll look into the massive market of plant foods. Soil is another factor of house-plant culture that all too often leaves people in a muddle. Yet none of these things—watering, feeding, or soil—should be a mystery and needn't be.

Watering Schedule

First, don't worry about what kind of water your city has and whether it's fit for plants or not. If you can drink it, plants will do just fine with it. The less scientific mumbo jumbo you allow yourself to absorb the better your plants will fare. What's important, however, is the *kind* of plant you have growing in what kind of light. So for the sake of simplicity we're going to have three watering schedules for plants in (1) *shady places,* (2) *bright places,* and (3) *sun.* No matter what kind of pot or its size, here are some general hints.

Plants in shade need a somewhat dry soil, which means watering *about once a week in spring and summer, about once every two weeks in fall, and once every three weeks in winter.* Doesn't sound like enough water to you? No, it won't be unless you remember that when you water, really water the plants; they should be soaked with each application. Sparse watering will kill them quickly, but a thorough soaking followed by the drying out time will suit them just fine. In shade, feeding should be kept to a minimum, with two applications of plant food, one in May and one in July; that's it!

For plants in a bright light, *water two to three times a week in spring and summer* and *once a week in fall and winter.* Again, soak them thoroughly; never give scanty waterings. You can also feed these plants more often than those in shade; give monthly feedings in March, April, May, June, July and August.

The sun lovers require the most attention and *need water every other day in spring and summer* and about *once a week in fall and winter.* These plants can tolerate feeding about twice a month in the warm months and an occasional application of food in, say, October. That's it! Well, not quite. These are general suggestions for various and sundry plants. Watering will also depend on just where a plant is—house, apartment, or office, for example. In the following chapters you'll find specific watering schedules for each group of plants.

Repotting

The subject of repotting plants is often glossed over in most garden books, but fresh soil with adequate nutrients can make the difference between a healthy plant or a sick one. Remember that plants in a confined area of soil in a pot quickly use up their nutrients in about five months in a bright place, about nine months in a shady location. Copious feeding is the prescribed panacea, but this is dangerous because excessive feeding can build up salts in soil that can harm plants. New soil at least once a year is a must. It takes time to repot a plant in a 6-, 8-, or 10-inch pot, but it's as necessary as watering. However, don't let your florist or nurseryman throw the fear of God into you about careful repotting and how to do it and so forth. It's simple. Remove the plant, take away old soil, and fill a new container with fresh soil. Just get it done! If you bruise the roots or even break a stem, no harm will be done; the plant will recover in short time. Repotting is not something for a specialist, but what you do with a plant after it gets fresh soil is! And herein is the secret of successful repotting. First, flood the plant with water the day you repot it. Do it after repotting and then again a few hours later and then, yes, again that night! The next day, above all protect the plant against intense sun or light. Keep it well shaded for a few days, and then put it in its permanent place. Remember, it's more what you do later with a plant than the actual repotting that will make the difference. If the plant doesn't seem to be getting on too well, give it more humidity. Put a plastic Baggie (propped on sticks) over it. If excessive condensation appears on the inside of the plastic, remove it occasionally.

Feeding

We've briefly discussed feeding, but now we really get into it. There are so many plant foods it boggles the mind. But you can be a loving gardener by just forgetting most of them. A plant basically needs nitrogen, phosphorous and potassium to grow. Nitrogen is the big food maker, phosphorous and potassium are necessary for strong stems and resistance to disease. Plants also need trace elements.

You can use the many man-made feeding products sold in bottles and packages at nurseries. The contents of N, P, P are marked on the package in percentages, for example 10–10–5, which means 10 percent nitrogen, 10 percent phosphorous, and 5 percent potassium. This is a fairly good commercial plant food for most plants, neither too strong nor too weak. Don't let anyone talk you into buying stronger solutions of 20–20–10 to make plants grow faster. Remember: Light is the governing factor, and no matter how much food you give, if light is minimal, the plant simply won't grow. It will die from excess feeding!

If the packaged commercial foods available in granular, soluble, or pellet forms overwhelm you, be an organic indoor gardener and give plants bone meal, which contains nitrogen and phosphorous, or cottonseed meal, which contains mainly nitrogen. (See chart at end of chapter.) I prescribe to this kind of feeding not because it may be better but because it is generally cheaper and I don't have to worry about numbers and percentages and soluble or granular or foliar foods hocus-pocus. Specific information of feeding is given with plant descriptions in later chapters.

Soils

There was a time when you could just take soil from your garden and use it for indoor plants. I still do on occasion, and plants grow fine in it. However, you may be in an area where soil is not good, so you should buy packaged soils. (I suppose people still mix their own soils, and this might make sense for greenhouse gardeners with many, many plants, but for the indoor gardener with a few plants, mixing your own soil is just that much more work for nothing.) There is an all-purpose pack-aged soil for most plants, but there are also special soils for African violets or philodendrons or cacti or gesneriads or this and that. Everyone wants to be a specialist, including the soil manufacturers. The main reason for the barrage of soils is that it makes you spend more money. If you have Afri-can-violet soil left over, you will hesitate to use it for philodendrons because you know there is spe-cial philodendron soil. Fie on such things—it only makes the manufacturer rich and you poor. Use the soil even if you have a cactus to plant. Speciali-zation is fine for brain surgery, but forget it for plant soils. Most are fine for all plants, so buy the most for the least and pot your plants. If they don't do well, it won't be because of the soil; it will be because of your culture.

One good tip: If you can, buy loose soil by the bushel from a good nursery or florist. It's hard to say whether they'll sell you this in this day and age, but if they do, get it. It's the same soil they use to grow their plants and thus has all necessary in-gredients for good growth. It's cheaper and better, however, than packaged soils, so that's why it may be hard to find.

Fertilizer Values
of Some Common Organic Substances

	Nitrogen (%)	Phosphorus (%)	Potassium (%)
Hoof and horn meal	13		
Blood meal	13		
Fish meals	9–14	3 or more	
Bone meal	3	12–24	
Cottonseed meal	7	1.1	1.36
Castor pomace	6		
Dry steer and cow manure	2		
Wood ashes			2.5–5
Alfalfa hay	2.35	.21	2

4 The House Gardener

If you own your own home or rent a house, chances are there's some space and some fairly good conditions for plants. In an apartment or office you are generally confined to one or two rooms, and heat is governed by other people, but in a home there are several places to move your plants if they don't do well in one area, and you control the heat. Bathrooms and kitchens are excellent places for plants because they're naturally more humid than other places in the home, and generally they aren't drafty. In the home there are also windowsills (at least one) where you can put some plants and of course, plants can decorate desks and tables.

The plants for the house are usually larger in size than apartment plants simply because there's more room. And treelike plants (one or two) can also be grown in the home. Since you have access to the furnace and can control heating, the plants generally will have fairly good conditions. The old saying that "If you're comfortable your plants will be" is worth repeating. Plants in hanging baskets can also decorate the scene, and terrariums are an excellent answer if you're a lazy gardener.

Caring for House Plants

Houses, like apartments, are apt to be dry, and the same cool-air vaporizer you buy when you have a cold makes an excellent source of humidity for house plants. When watering plants, soak them thoroughly, and if light is fairly good, water them three times a week and feed lightly once a month, except in winter. Large plants in containers over 12 inches will need water less than plants in smaller containers, but those miniatures in 3- or 4-inch pots can use water every day.

As a rule, it's a good idea to group house plants, that is, five or six in one area on a table near a window, on a salvage teacart in the dining room, or on a plant stand. Watering is then a breeze, and you're not apt to forget one plant hidden in a remote corner of the room.

If you're home all day, water plants in mid-morning when temperatures are leveling out in your home; this isn't mandatory, just a suggestion. I have a friend who always waters his plants at night (contrary to all garden-book advice); he has a jungle.

Once a month soak pot plants to the rim in a sink or tub of water for about two hours or until you see air bubbles on top of the soil. This leaches out excess salts and thoroughly moistens all parts of the soil. Spray-mist foliage with water whenever you think of it to add humidity and refresh the plants. And do wipe leaves with a damp cloth when you do your regular household dusting because it keeps pores open and plants healthy.

As mentioned in other parts parts of this book, move plants around until you find a place they like. Avoid drafts and sudden temperature fluctuations; select appropriate places for your plants where there's good ventilation but no sneaky drafts that can wilt a dieffenbachia faster than you can boil an egg.

Use plants as decorator pieces; for example, if you need a vertical accent, select a tall rubber tree or a dizygotheca. Where mass is wanted to fill a void, use rosette plants like bromeliads or bushy ones like pittosporum. When there are several plants in a room, try to balance the setting with a few small plants, a large one, and so forth. Use large plants as you would furniture and the smaller ones as accessories. It's always nice to enter a room of plants for there's a fresh green feeling that's cheerful to the soul and that makes for better conversation.

If certain plants become straggly (some philodendrons and such can), have no qualms about pruning and grooming them. Removing a leaf or a stem here or there won't harm a plant and indeed might help it because new growth will be encouraged. And finally, if a plant becomes badly infested with insects or disease, discard it! Yes, this is cruel, but it's far better to save other plants in the house than to perpetuate the plague.

Plants for the House

Begonias

The large group of begonias (about 200 in the family) offers the house owner a veritable treasure of plants that will adjust to cool, dark, dry rooms.

The rhizomatous types, with thick aerial roots, and the hirsute (hairy) types seem to do the best because they have some protection to withstand heat and cold and can take dryness too. And if anyone tells you begonias aren't pretty, tell them to look again. It's all a matter of selection, and some have magnificent foliage and pretty flowers. As with all large plant groups though, avoid some species, including rexes and angel-wings, which just take too much time and care for the average person.

Here are the six best begonias I've grown throughout the years. These were the top performers, and if you grow them, you'll get very attached to them, old-fashioned though they may appear. (But a little bit of nostalgia never hurt anyone.) Grow the first three begonias somewhat moist; let the last three allow to dry out between waterings. All will succeed admirably in bright light or even shade.

Begonia boweri (eye-lash begonia) is rhizomatous. It's a charming plant, to about 20 inches, with delicate green leaves stitched with black. Very decorative and worthy of a place in any house.

B. crestubruchi (lettuce-leaf begonia) really does look like its common name, and is a tough indoor plant to beat for beauty. The leaves are heavily ruffled, twisted, and yellow-green, and plants are massive and beautiful.

B. maphil, sometimes called Cleopatra begonia, is a star performer indoors, with colorful star-shaped leaves splashed with dark brown, gold and chartreuse; enough color for anyone.

B. prunifolia can become a glorious sight, with cupped, bunchy, and lush dark green leaves, and will even throw some white flowers if you're very, very good with it.

B. scharffiana offers green-red plush leaves and a hairy root stock that climbs on the soil, sort of a sculptural plant growth. Well worth your attention.

**Eyelash Begonia
(Begonia boweri)**

B. viaudi is a wooly white charmer, with green leaves on top and red underneath, all covered with fine white little hairs. A bearded beauty.

Gesneriads

A flowering gesneriad that will brighten your dullest days is *Kohleria amabilis*. It is a regal plant, with upright growth, large dark green velvety leaves; occasionally, but not often, it will surprise you with some funnel-shaped pink flowers. Keep plant reasonably moist and in good light.

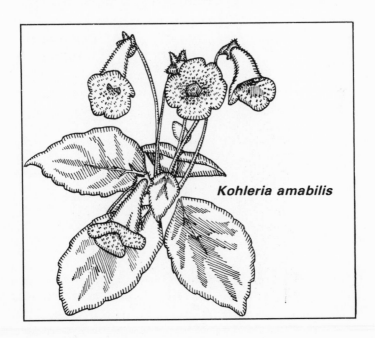

Kohleria amabilis

Another gesneriad worthy of mention is *Columnea arguta*, a low, light, level plant that has trailing small dark green leaves, a cascade of beauty. Huge salmon-red flowers dot the plant in warm weather. Keep evenly moist, and do select this trailer rather than aeschynanthus (the lipstick vine), which most dealers will try to sell you in its place. The profitable (for the nurseryman) lipstick vine is trouble because it invariably attracts mealybugs.

Coffee plants are recently available; the one known by the botanical name of *Coffea arabica* is the *real* coffee plant. Don't expect to go to the kitchen in the morning and grind your own though —this plant is for beautiful shiny green foliage

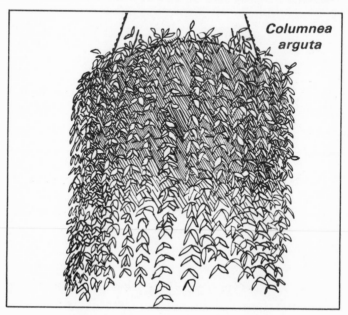

Columnea arguta

Coffee Plant
(*Coffea arabica*)

only. It's well worth its price because it grows into a lovely bushy foliage plant that will warm the heart on the coldest days. It doesn't mind cool night temperatures at all and will fare just fine in shade.

Cycads

Mention the name cycad and people will look at you askance, but learn the name well because this family offers some plants for untenable places. Best described as perhaps somewhere between a fern and a palm, cycads are the oldest plants known to man, and you'll be glad you met them. Just keep them somewhat evenly moist in any dark corner and you'll bless the day you found them. Included in this group is the sago palm *(Cycas revoluta)*. Buy big plants rather than skimpy ones because they'll be well worth your money. They do grow slowly (perhaps a frond a year), but they're so beautiful and indestructible that they deserve a place at home. One of the best, if you can locate it, is *Dion edule,* which looks like a rosette of leaves sitting on a pineapple. The foliage is almost plastic in appearance, but it's as real as can be, and the fronds are feathery.

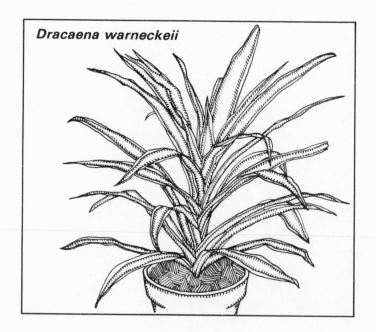

Dracaena warneckeii

Dracaenas

There are plants and there are plants, and dracaenas are perhaps the gardener's dream. They perform admirably with little care and can tolerate darkness with abandonment. *D. warneckeii,* when grown several to a pot, is handsome, with dark green leaves striped white; it needs to be almost wet. Needing drying out between waterings is the decorator plant *D. marginata,* with sword-shaped green leaves on long stalks. And not to be forgotten because it grows into a lovely tree is *D. massangeana,* which likes an intermediate moist soil. Keep clipping as it keeps growing and you'll have a splendid tree that will live for a long time.

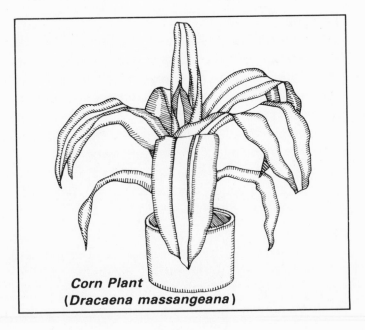

Corn Plant
(*Dracaena massangeana*)

Dieffenbachias

It's hard to discuss the next group of plants (dieffenbachias) because either they don't like me or I don't like them, but through the years I've found them almost impossible to grow for more than a few years. They invariably get leggy, lose leaves at the bottom, and branch and twist into contorted shapes. When you think you finally have a statuesque plant, you end up with a bare-branched sculpture when they drop their leaves from a draft. Yes, these plants are highly sensitive to drafts and fluctuating temperatures, but *D. amoena* and *D. picta*, if you can take the trouble, are beautiful additions to a room.

Hibiscus

For pure beauty and color it's hard to beat a large pot of *Hibiscus rosa-sinensis* in the living room. These lovelies can grow quite tall, and most start blooming with saucer-sized flowers in winter, a pleasant sight, with one flower following another for weeks. Don't be panic-stricken if at times the plant dies down and then starts growing again; this seems to be its natural pattern indoors. Give hibiscus buckets of water and more warmth than most plants mentioned in this section.

Philodendrons

The workhorses of the indoor plant world are the philodendrons. If chosen carefully, they're truly fine plants, but all too often the varieties offered by florists and nurseries are the bad rather than the good ones. But the good ones do outnumber the bad ones, so if you can't find any of the following at local sources, order them by mail. It's worth it because some philodendrons are just gorgeous, and that's not a word I use often.

If you want to fall in love fast, look for a mature specimen of *P. soderoi,* with large heart-shaped dark green leaves. It sort of branches and makes a splendid indoor plant in even a dark spot. Wash leaves frequently, and keep soil good and moist. Another lovely in this chorus lineup of philodendrons is *P. bipinnatifidum,* with large, deeply cut, crinkly green leaves. A mature plant is well worth the space and is dramatic. Like most philoden-

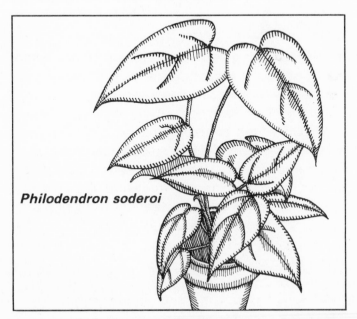

Philodendron soderoi

Philodendron bipinnatifidum

drons mentioned here, this one needs space and can grow quite tall with little coaxing from you. Just keep it well watered. A dark place is ideal for this jungle beauty.

A solid-leaved philodendron is *P. cannifolium*, with arrow-shaped foliage of dark lustrous green. This plant can take untenable conditions and still survive. Ideally it likes good moisture and humidity but will settle for less; you can't find a nicer plant. One of the self-heading philodendrons (those that look like cabbages) is *P. wendlandii*. This is a mammoth rosette of huge and solid bright green leaves and makes a stellar living room accent. Search for it because it's worth it; it's different and indestructible. Keep it evenly moist.

Avoid, if you can, philodendrons such as *P. cordatum* and the ubiquitous *Monstera deliciosa* (commonly called Swiss cheese philodendron). This one always gets straggly, and although it makes a big impression when you first see it, after the first year it looks like a fading star (and you know what they look like).

Palms

Palms for the house can't be overlooked. These plants naturally rest in winter and grow in spring and summer and so are ideal for the home. Furthermore, palms like shade and do very well in it if they have some good air circulation. Most palms like to dry out between watering. One of the best palms is *Rhapis excelsa,* with bright green fronds. It's a really good low bushy palm that can take abuse if necessary. The howea palms are other good candidates, although be wary here because some are pygmy variety and will never grow more than three feet. Most are fine though and will break a few fronds a year. Howeas are a tropical explosion for a few cups of water every other day.

Ferns

If ferns are your favorites, and they are mine, you have a wide array to choose from, including the Boston ferns. These do quite well in shady, good-circulating-air places, but why not look for some different ferns? Davallias are lacy and lovely, and woodwardias are big and bold and as tough as they come. Avoid the varieties 'Fluffy Ruffles' and 'Rooseveltii' in the Boston clan. They've earned a reputation in my house as temperamental, whereas other ferns flourish. Also stay away from the beautiful adiantums (maidenhairs), which are tough to grow, and the tropical platyceriums, which need a Florida setting to perform, if they ever do. (See Chapter 8 for a more detailed discussion of ferns.)

Hoyas

If you come across a good mature species of *Hoya carnosa,* the wax plant, grab it. It can be an outstanding house plant, although the small ones aren't worth the time it takes to grow them to perfection. They're difficult, but the bigger ones seem to have more timber and can really provide a lovely display. Hoyas are viners, so be prepared, and also be prepared for the scented waxy white magnificent flower clusters that appear even away from windows. Keep these plants almost dry all year for the best results, and never, never part with a mature hoya if you have one. They are like fine silver: always wanted..

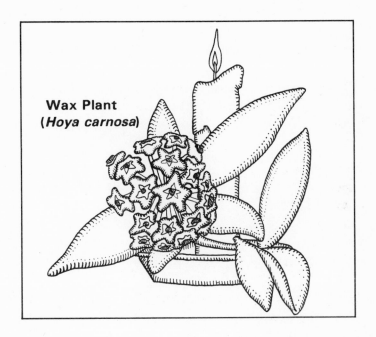

Wax Plant
(*Hoya carnosa*)

5 The Apartment Gardener

Through the years I've had small apartments in Chicago and California. The first thing I do when I move into an apartment—and I'm not alone in this —is to buy some pot plants to brighten the setting. It's ironical that small dark apartments where we need green plants the most to keep us in touch with nature, have the toughest conditions for plants. First, unless you're in a very new building, heat is controlled by the building owner; heat quickly diminishes after 10:00 P.M., when most apartments are at about 60° F. By law, heat is required to start at 6:30 A.M., gradually peaking at 8:00 or so. These are hardly ideal conditions. And to further compound and confuse the apartment gardener, the areas where you'll be growing plants are quite dry. This lack of humidity can, above all, quickly desiccate a plant.

So how do you cope with these conditions and still have some green plants? The answer is selection and then proper care under the conditions you have. It's not difficult, and in this chapter I hope to show you how to turn your dark apartment into a sylvan one.3

Caring for Apartment Plants

When you get that charming plant home you set it on a desk or table or on a windowsill; in two days you're despairing because the plant seems to be dying. Don't panic. Remember that the plant has, until it entered your domain, been grown under ideal greenhouse conditions: lots of rich moisture, warmth, and pampering. So the initial shock of your apartment is anything but a welcome place for plants. But plants, like people, are quite adaptable and will adjust to your conditions although they do need some help.

When you get your plants home, don't immediately set them in a bright or sunny place that's piping warm. (Brick apartment buildings can be quite warm in the middle of the day.) Pick a somewhat dark, cool place, and let the plant rest there a few days. Then start routine watering and care.

If you've lived in your apartment for a few months, you pretty much know its climate. It may be cool in the morning and night, but warm during the day. This is fine because many plants will accept these conditions. They naturally like a lower temperature at night than during the day. Try to put the plant where it will get some sunlight; if this isn't possible, because of small windows or natural light being obscured by other buildings, select the brightest place possible. For the first few weeks observe the plant and how it looks. Are leaves wilted, stems wan? If so, move it to another location. It may have been in a draft, or a door closing and opening near it may have caused havoc. For example, there's one bad spot in my kitchen: On this high shelf I tried several plants, namely, ferns and philodendrons, and all died. It took me several days to realize the trouble was the automatic dishwasher located directly below the shelf. Heat rises, so whenever I did the dishes in the washer the plant suffered greatly because vast quantities of hot air were being directed at it. Look out for small things like this; they can make a difference in successful plant growth.

If you're working all week, set a care schedule that doesn't interfere with your routine. Water the plants twice a week when you have your coffee, and let it go at that. But come the weekend, if you want green healthy plants, you're going to have to do something for them, including:

1. Soaking the plant in the sink for a few hours (about once a month)
2. Wiping leaves with a damp cloth
3. Applying a light plant food (see previous information)
4. Removing dead leaves and stems
5. Inspecting for insects
6. Repotting, if necessary

This may seem like a lot of care, but while the plant soaks in the sink it can be wiped with a damp cloth and groomed and inspected for insects—a mere ten minutes of your time.

If humidity is low in your apartment, and most apartments do have terrible humidity conditions, set up a tray with gravel in it. Keep the gravel moist, and set potted plants on it. And last but not least, spray plants with water twice a week when you water them. If you follow the above hints and select plants from the following list, your apartment, no matter how dark or dry, should be festooned with healthy plants.

Plants for the Apartment

For years I've kept in mind a list of house plants that can, if necessary, adapt to untenable conditions, and still survive. These are what I call my apartment plants. They may not be unique or exotic, but they're robust plants and are available in practically any garden center or plant shop.

A very good apartment plant that can take dry atmosphere and low humidity and still be pretty is the century plant, *Agave americana marginata.* The rosette shape is pleasing; the leaves are handsome, dark green lined yellow; and the plant can become a lovely decorator accent when it's big.

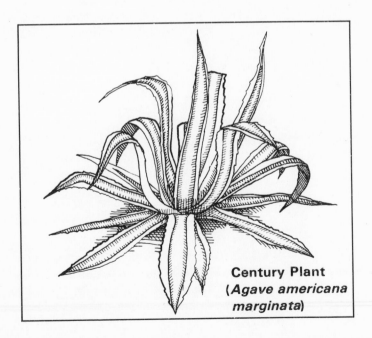

**Century Plant
(*Agave americana marginata*)**

Accepting north light but liking west light better, the century plant should be grown more often, even the small plants look nice. Keep the soil somewhat dry, and if your agave suddenly blooms, don't panic—these plants do bloom about every seven years, not every 100 years!

Once aglaonemas (Chinese evergreens) were grown only if you *had* to grow them (a gift perhaps). Now, because of so many new lovely varieties with variegated leaves, they're worth everyone's attention, and they're easy to grow. Indeed, well-grown species with bushy habits can be quite appealing. These plants like water, so keep soil moist; otherwise they need shade and an occa-

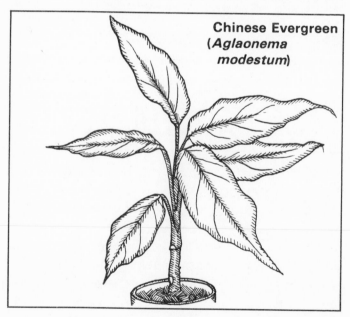

Chinese Evergreen (*Aglaonema modestum*)

sional wiping of leaves with a damp cloth.

Looking more like a fern than a lily (which it is), the emerald fern, *Asparagus sprengeri,* is a gem for all seasons. This filmy vision of greenness should be a favorite house plant because it grows lush and large and will fill its pot. If you want a big plant, start even a tiny guy in an 8-inch pot and let it go. This plant likes lots of water and a bright place, but it will readily accept coolness at night. At Christmas the plant bears little flowers and lovely red berries that really make it a find among plants. Don't be talked into a recent introduction called *Asparagus plumosus.* It has plumes of green and is much more difficult to grow than *Asparagus sprengeri.*

Do you like pineapples? You can grow the commercial pineapple *Ananas comosus.* If you're stubborn, you can start it from scratch from the top of a pineapple, but if you haven't the time, buy a small plant. It has grayish green straplike leaves and, like most bromeliads, grows easily. Give it a bright place, and water it occasionally. Nature does the rest.

Want a banana in your apartment? Well, now there's no need not to have one. *Musa nana* is the little banana, and though it won't bear fruit it does have interesting spatula-shaped lathe green leaves that make it worth space. It likes some warmth and frequent waterings. Growing on a single trunk, this is a good apartment plant where there is little natural light.

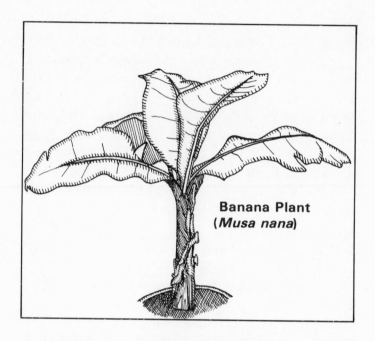

**Banana Plant
(*Musa nana*)**

A large plant, to 36 inches, *Aechmea chantini* will absolutely put envy in your guest's eyes. This fine bromeliad has handsome leaves banded gray and green and bears, even in apartments, an exotic flower head of yellow and red. It's an impressive plant and included here to impress. Give it bright light or shade, and keep the vase filled with water. This is an exotic and regal beauty for even the darkest apartment.

The corkscrew pine *(Pandanus veitchii)* has long been a favorite of mine and seems to love apartment living. It thrives on steam heat and is a handsome rosette of graceful, long, tapering, and toothed green-and-white leaves (resembles an

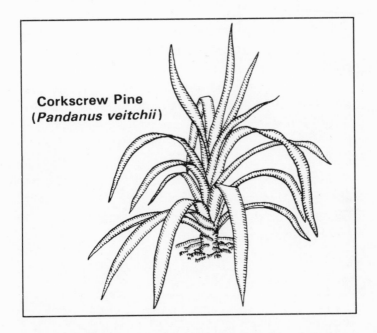

**Corkscrew Pine
(*Pandanus veitchii*)**

aechmea). The plant grows quickly into a decorator piece; even a seedling will, in three years, be big enough to decorate a corner. Keep it somewhat dry rather than sopping wet, and occasionally wipe leaves with damp cloth. My plant of the month!

Here's a fern that will survive dark, cool, and dry apartments: *Blechnum brasiliense.* The name sounds terrible, but it's a stiff and fronded robust grower unlike the Boston fern, which needs some pampering. It will grow in a north light, but you'll have to keep the soil evenly moist all year. This is a nice fern and one of the few that really require little care.

The darling of the plant world, *Tolmiea menziesii*, also called piggyback or pick-a-back plant, depending upon whom you talk to, is included for people who like to pamper a plant. This water guzzler wilts quicker than ice cream in August if you forget it even one day. It's a lush ball of light green leaves and invariably dies on me. (I have 300 plants; and piggyback is not one of my favorites!)

Recommended for offices and equally good for apartments is the Norfolk pine, *Araucaria excelsa*. Give it a bright place and keep the soil evenly moist. Always good.

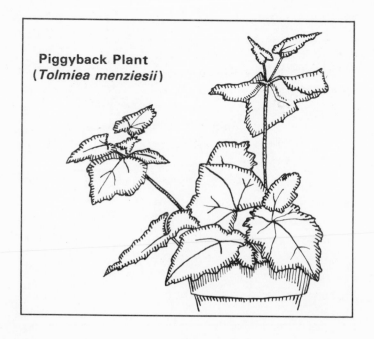

**Piggyback Plant
(*Tolmiea menziesii*)**

Some people will tell you that the ti-plant, *Cordyline terminalis,* grows only in water, but it does even better in soil. This plant has lovely dark green, red-edged leaves that are graceful and lovely. Large plants are beautiful to see, and because you're going to grow this with love and care, strive for a large one in an 8-inch pot. Keep it evenly moist, somewhat warm, and enjoy it. This is a good apartment dweller that revels in darkness and adds a note of exotica to the place; it's nice to have around on those gray winter mornings.

The crown of thorns may sound too religious for

Norfolk Pine (*Araucaria excelsa*)

Crown of Thorns
(*Euphorbia splendens*)

you, but *Euphorbia splendens bojeri* is a little bit of heaven because it blooms indoors in little light with lovely scarlet flowers. The stems are thorny and might draw blood; but this is still a fine if hazardous, plant. The plant has a nice branching effect and fares well in most all light situations, although in bright light it will have a bumper harvest. Keep this gem somewhat dry, and inspect frequently for mealybugs, which find the crown of thorns delectable. There are several varieties, so don't get confused—you want the one with tiny and round dark green leaves and red blooms.

I don't know why people grow ivy, but they do, so it must be included here. *Hedera helix* (English ivy) has been a favorite room plant for years, which really puzzles me because this ubiquitous plant invariably attracts red spiders even under ideal conditions and is always a bother. If you must have one, keep the plant as cool as possible, and keep soil moist to the touch.

A charming apartment plant is *Kalanchoe tomentosa* (panda plant), which is recommended because it's gray-green in color rather than all green and is somewhat furry and different. It has a charm of its own, and, like most succulents, it doesn't demand too much attention. Let the soil dry out between waterings, and give it bright light. Nice to touch on sad days, the panda plant is okay.

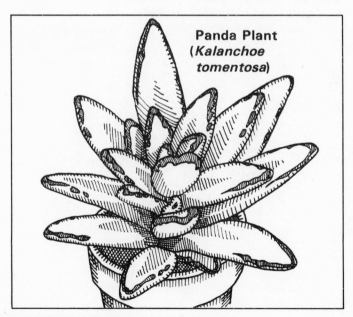

Panda Plant (*Kalanchoe tomentosa*)

If you can afford a palm, don't be talked into anything but *Chamaedorea erumpens,* the bamboo palm. Other palms are apt to be a pain to apartment dwellers always on the go, but the bamboo palm can make it on its own with little care from you. I think it has a secret pact with someone up there! It will be happy if you're gone all day and not pampering it. The plant has thick dark green fronds and grows quickly. Splurge (they're costly) and enjoy one. Keep it well watered all year except in winter, when it can be carried on the dry side. A stellar performing apartment plant you will bless me for.

Bamboo Palm (*Chamaedorea erumpens*)

Want to fill a lot of space in a few months? Try the Swedish ivy *(Plectranthus coleoides)*. It grows like a weed and is an excellent hanging plant with rounded, somewhat succulent, leaves, bushy and nice. New species, such as velvet plectranthus and little-leaved plectranthus keep appearing, but for safety and ease of culture stick to the original *Plectranthus coleoides*. Give it water a few times a week, and spray it occasionally with a mist of water. Watch for mealybugs, which like the leaves.

Here's a plant with a terrible name: *Siderasis fuscata*. However, this leafy gem does very well in apartments. The leaves are covered with minute

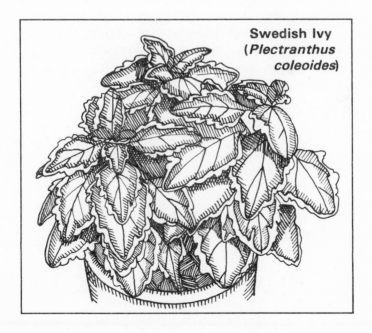

Swedish Ivy
(*Plectranthus*
***coleoides*)**

hairs, but in a proper white container siderasis thrives and looks appealing. It likes to be somewhat dry, and try not to splotch leaves with water. Never an obtrusive plant; you'll like this one because it survives even in darkness.

A tiny, delicate tree for the living room can sometimes make the day for you. *Punica granatum nana,* the pomegranate, is a delightful, appealing charmer, with tiny leaves and branching growth. The tree likes bright light and regular waterings. Give it a try, but don't expect the world. It's simply an adequate plant—no more, no less.

Oops—almost forgot mother-in-law's tongue (sansevieria). Yes, they are indestructible and now there are several excellent varieties such as *S. trifasciata 'Hahni'* that are splendid color. Indeed, I wouldn't be surprised if they change the common name. Water sansevieria sparingly, but do wipe leaves occasionally with a damp cloth. Please, no sun, or they will really talk back to you.

9 The Office Gardener

One of the enjoyments of being a garden writer is visiting editors' offices, where there are always plants. Even at windows obscured by the Pan Am building (New York), there are plants to brighten the working space, and I've noticed that some grow better than others. Since you spend every weekday at the place where you work, there's nothing wrong in having some greenery for gray days when the weather or the boss gets you down. Also, it has been proven that people work better with plants around. So if you need some new enthusiasm, tell your boss to get you a few plants.

The care of plants in the office is exactly the opposite of those at home. In the office you can care for plants during the week, but on weekends and holidays (and so many fall on Monday now it means three days of no care) you must find ingenious ways of keeping your plants growing. Furthermore, such house-plant tricks as soaking plants in sinks may be impossible; however, other methods are available.

Humidity in offices is generally better than humidity in apartments. New heating and humidifying systems are often part of the office furnace system, and these help you and your plants. Indeed, it seems that I've seen healthier plants in offices than I have in homes. Also, until recently office fluorescent lights were left on for twenty-four hours, a great help in supplying sufficient light for plant growth. And, air conditioning, contrary to most beliefs, helps rather than hinders plants.

The main problem with office plants seems to be ventilation: Offices generally are tightly closed. Whether this is a directive from the upper regions or a matter of someone not having time to open a window, I don't know, but opening the window slightly, even in winter, will greatly help the plants, although it might anger the superintendent, who'll say that all the heat on the fortieth floor is escaping because you have your window open. Tell him to look at the lovely plants and be quiet.

Caring for Office Plants

Assuming that humidity is adequate (a small hygrometer will tell you this), water your office plants every other day during the week, with special attention to Friday waterings. Then allow some water to remain in the saucer or dish. (Self-watering pots are available, but it seems that few people have them or want to cope with them.) Keep a small spray-bottle on hand; at lunchtime or during coffee-break, mist the foliage daily.

In winter, artificial heat is at its highest, so plants will get dryer quicker than you think. This is *not* the time to stop watering plants; keep watering on a twice-a-week schedule.

Always inspect plants as you take a break from work or stretch your legs. If you see any signs of insects, use an aerosol house-plant pesticide. I know poisons are out in today's ecology, and that's how it should be, but in an office or home, spraying a few plants with some pesticide is not considered foolish. You may also use systemic insecticides; they come in granular form. Just sprinkle them on soil and water, and plants will be protected from some insects for about three months.

In the office, don't grow rampant growers such as tradescantias or the ubiquitous *Philodendron cordatum* because these plants soon become straggly and ill-kempt without constant attention and they must be potted frequently. Stick to handsome, bushy plants or rosette types that never get out of bounds.

Repotting a plant isn't difficult, but it is awkward to get soil and equipment into the office. Thus sometimes it's best just to dig out the top two to three inches of soil and replace it with fresh soil. Feed with a standard 10–10–5 plant food once a month all year, except in December and January.

Plants for the Office

Following is a selection of good office denizens that will brighten your working day. There's more of a selection here because, quite frankly, office conditions in most cases are better than apartment conditions for plants.

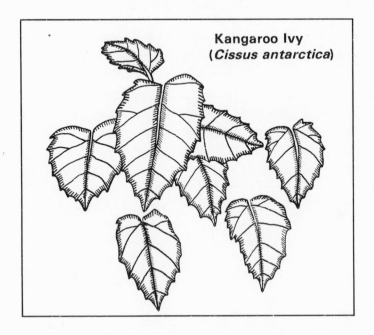

Kangaroo Ivy
(*Cissus antarctica*)

The kangaroo ivy *(Cissus antartica)* is neither too large nor too small and is rich green in color, good for any spot in the office. It can grow almost (but not ideally) in the dark if it must. The scalloped leaves are larger than those of grape ivy *(C. rhombifolia)*, and the plant rarely gets leggy like the latter. By nature it's a climber and rather fast growing, so it always brings satisfaction because new leaves appear regularly. The kangaroo vine takes a great deal of water, grows in even north light, and is rarely troubled by insects. All in all, this is a stalwart addition to the office.

If you want to look like a gardener without lifting

your finger and impress your co-workers, grow *Neoregelia carolinae.* This bromeliad is a member of the pineapple family but looks more like a rosette of lovely shiny and attractive green leaves. In a way it's a fraud though; it rarely grows more than a leaf a year and will stay as you got it for some time. But because it requires little light and is so amenable, you'll love it. Keep it in a porous soil, and always try to have some water in the center of the plant or vase. And maybe yours will grow more rapidly than my plants if there's enough typing and calculator sounds to vibrate its foliage. (Don't laugh; some people play music for their plants.)

If there's a shelf at the window or a spot for a hanging plant, consider the pencil cactus *(Rhip-*

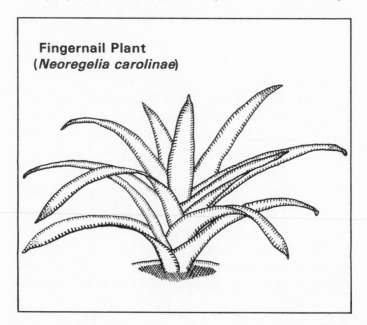

**Fingernail Plant
(*Neoregelia carolinae*)**

salis paradoxa). The plant looks like an elongated string of green pencils and might be right at home in the office. It's not spectacular, but a good full plant has a certain unique jungle effect. Give it enough water to keep soil lightly moist, but do caress its leaves with a damp cloth occasionally, but not too fervently.

For a small space, say on your desk amidst the papers and pencils, *Haworthia fasciata* is your plant. It's a gray-green rosette of succulent leaves and can grow for years in a 4-inch pot unconscious of your or its surroundings, but perfectly happy. Its texture and shape make it worthwhile, and it needs only occasional watering to be content. Like most plants mentioned here, it will adapt to less than good conditions and be with you a long time. If it gets to be too long a time, give it to someone because it's quite charming.

There's nothing wrong with a little sculpture in the office, and *Agave fasciata* can masquerade as a piece of carved jade. It's a magnificent, medium-sized plant with a tight crown of angular succulent leaves penciled white. Impressive? Yes. And not easy to find but always available from mail-order dealers; it's well worth its extra cost. Get a mature plant about 10 inches across and be the envy of the office force. This plant likes some bright light and occasional waterings, but nothing much else. It will adapt to office temperatures, whether they be desert-hot in summer (when the air conditioning is broken) or cool in winter (when radiators don't work).

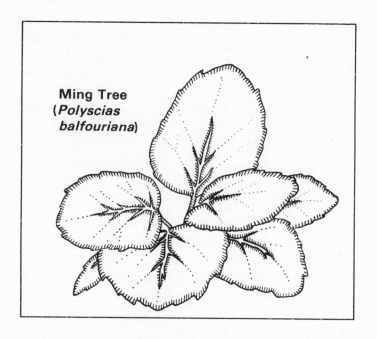

Ming Tree
(*Polyscias
balfouriana*)

Polyscias balfouriana is a filmy, lacy, unusual plant with a trunklike stem, so if you want a miniature tree in your office, this one is for you. It's not as easy to get along with as others in this list because it tends to need some talking to to make it feel at home, but once established it will grow quickly and impress everyone with its bright green ferny leaves. Keep this one moist at all times and away from drafts.

If your office isn't large enough for a Christmas tree, try the Norfolk pine *(Auracaria excelsa),* which looks somewhat like a miniature holiday tree. It's pyramidal in growth, piney looking, and adds a nice note of green to concrete buildings. It will never become too large, and it certainly isn't exotic, but it's still worth its space because it grows with just routine water and never attracts insects.

The velvet plant *(Gynura sarmentosa)* has become popular lately, and although I think it looks straggly, you may think its trailing habit and dark green red-lined leaves are just the things for a tired office area. It will need plenty of water and a shady place; if you don't mind being grown out of your space, give it a try.

A bromeliad with rosettes of powdery green striped leaves, *Aechmea fasciata*, the silver urn plant, deserves a star for performance, even in the

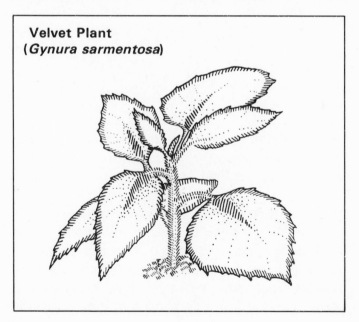

**Velvet Plant
(*Gynura sarmentosa*)**

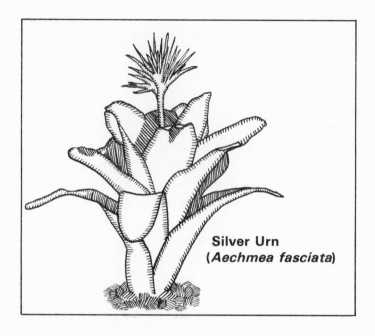

**Silver Urn
(*Aechmea fasciata*)**

darkest dance hall. And it will bloom like a star too, even in north light, so it's well worth your attention. The plant is somewhat large, to about 24 inches, but because it offers so much, I recommend it. Keep the vase filled with water (and little cut flowers if you like), and enjoy the whole scene.

Smaller than *A. fasciata* but just as lovely and amenable is *A. racinae,* a somewhat vaselike plant with dark green shiny leaves and flower bracts that will knock you out: They're vibrant red and black and last longer than a dozen expensive roses. This plant is small, so it can be tucked away in any corner, where it will demand attention. Like the

other bromeliads in this book, it needs little attention to prosper.

The color of the foliage, dark green, makes the
wandering Jew *(Zebrina pendula)* worth space.
And too, it does grow quickly into a lush plant but
can occasionally become temperamental and just
die back from drafts or changes in temperature.
Still, because it generally does well, it's ok. Do
remember though that it loves water and virtually
sops it up, so every time you have a coffee-break,
give the plant a break and water it. Then hope it
doesn't grow you out of office space.

Here's a plant with water reservoirs in tuberlike

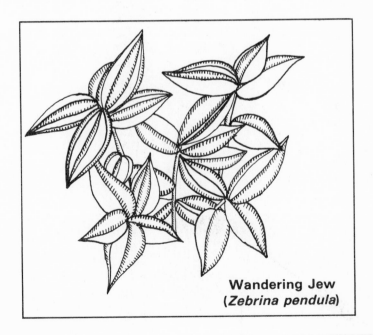

**Wandering Jew
(*Zebrina pendula*)**

roots that can store water, if necessary, so this is for you if you forget your duties. This plant is called *Chlorophytum elatum* and has many common names: spider plant, aeroplane plant, friendship plant, and so on. It's a grassy green charming plant that grows and grows in bright light only. Give it routine care, and don't feel guilty if you forget to water it.

The jade tree *(Crassula argentea)*, around for a long time, is a tough house plant that performs equally well in the office. It has round, succulent, gray-green leaves and a good woody stem I think is most attractive. It needs very little care, just enough water to keep soil evenly moist. All in all

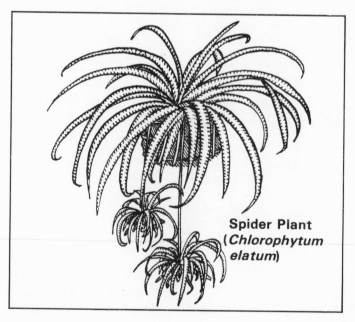

**Spider Plant
(*Chlorophytum
elatum*)**

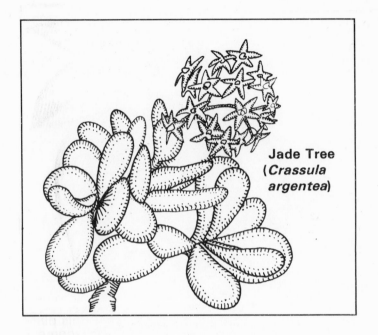

Jade Tree
(*Crassula argentea*)

this is a good subject for even the nongardener.

I like large-leaved plants because they look lush; *Hoffmannia ghiesbreghtii* is just that. The dark leaves are beautifully veined, and although it's a heat-loving plant, its different growth habit and tropical looks make it a candidate for the office. The plant never gets too large but rather (and I think it nice) gets bushy and can be on your desk, bookcase, or wherever to add a note of the jungle. Hoffmannia likes a moist soil and warmth, so act accordingly. You'll probably have to order this one by mail, but its different enough to warrant the postage.

Better known as pothos, which is just as bad as

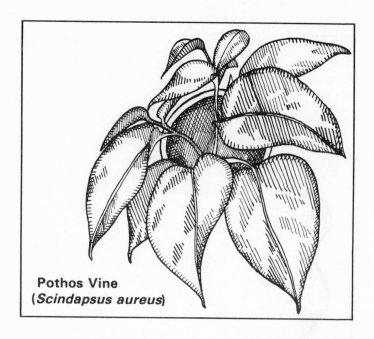

**Pothos Vine
(*Scindapsus aureus*)**

its botanical name, *Scindapsus aureus,* this plant has never done much for me except become a tangle of leaves. But some people like that and grow it with passion. The heart-shaped foliage, blotched with yellow or white, is quite attractive, but the plant grows like there's no tomorrow and becomes straggly. Pinch it back occasionally to show who is boss. There's no need for cultural notes because this one could grow in a cave if it had to.

Rarely seen but available, and certainly worth space in an office where there's shade and coolness, is *Spathiphyllum clevelandii,* sometimes called white flag plant. It's a lovely bouquet of greenery, with long, dark green tapering leaves. It becomes a somewhat larger plant than most listed here, but could be placed on the floor or on a tiny pedestal. It will grow well if you keep a finger on the soil. It never wants to be too wet or too dry, only slightly moist.

Syngonium podophyllum is called the arrowhead plant, but grows like a weed. The foliage is arrow-shaped and shiny green and may be bushy or more of a climber, depending upon how it reacts to your vibrations. Equally happy in north, west, or east light, the arrowhead can give much pleasure for little cost and does well in most situa-

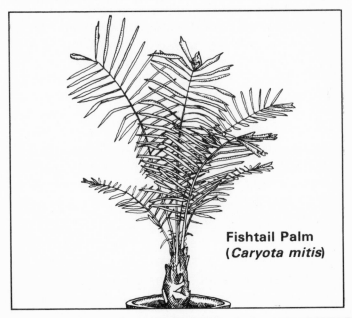

Fishtail Palm (*Caryota mitis*)

tions. In a 6-inch pot it will charm you for months, maybe years, and will also keep you running to the water spigot every day.

Do you like palms? If so, here's one for the office: the fishtail palm *(Caryota mitis)*. Overlooked for years, this little, shiny, green-leaved gem can glow like a fish and become a lush lovely plant. Keep it evenly moist.

If I left philodendrons out of this section, I would be berated by all philly lovers, so here goes. For the office try some of the smaller philodendrons like *P. cordatum* or *P. hastatum*. The former has heart-shaped leaves; the latter has arrow-shaped, dark green foliage. Both are climbers that tend to get leggy, so that's why I recommend them with discretion. Quite frankly, philodendrons are lovely but need some pampering. Keep them moist if you have one, and forget what I said if you love them.

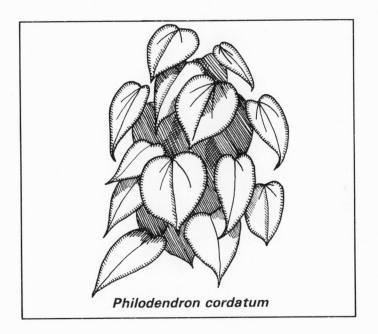

Philodendron cordatum

7 Flowering Plants That Can Take It

For years African violets have been the leader of plants that can provide colorful blossoms indoors with little light. Few other plants were ever mentioned, but there are many others in the same family (gesneriads) that will bloom indoors in less than good light. Smithianthas, with red flowers, and kohlerias and columneas, bright with orange blooms, are only a few. Orchids, so long considered conservatory plants, are now popular house plants, and in this huge family of some 35,000 species there are many, many fine lovely orchids that will bear flowers in shady places.

Old standbys for indoor gardeners are the fine robust cacti and succulents. These plants too will grace indoors with colorful bloom, without too much light. So if you've been thinking you can't grow flowering plants, come out of the dark and look at all these fine possibilities to tickle your fingers and delight the eye.

Flowering plants in bloom are colorful and charming, beautiful accents for the indoor garden. There are thousands of flowering plants that can be grown at home, but perhaps gesneriads, orchid cacti, and orchids are the most showy and the best to have. Many were once conservatory plants but have now taken their rightful place indoors. Some, of course, remain solely for greenhouse growing, but these are exceptions rather than the rule.

Flowering plants offer a great deal for little money. Kohlerias, dripping with scarlet bloom, are stunning coffee-table accents; orchids, with an incredible variety of dramatic flowers, give an area a tropical effect. And the mammoth flowers of epiphyllums always cause comment.

Although some flowering plants need infinite care—daily watering, exacting humidity—there are many others that thrive with little more care than the culture you use for foliage plants. And some are easier to grow. Orchid cactus have their peak bloom in May and June. Many gesneriads are in full color from April to September, and orchids round out the year with fall- and winter-flowering plants.

Gesneriads

This overlooked group includes some fine indoor subjects, with flowers perhaps prettier than those of African violets. Kohlerias laden with brilliantly colored bell-shaped flowers are stunning at the window. Gloxinias, easy to grow and very floriferous, are certainly exciting plants. Smithianthas, columneas, and achimenes are some of the many other gesneriads. We'll discuss many of these here; we're not omitting African violets out of preference but merely because of space (there are many fine books on these plants).

Like orchids, many of the gesneriads come from the tropics, that is, dark, moist conditions. But this doesn't mean they must be grown in excessive heat and humidity. Most are comfortable if you are, and average home conditions suit them well. Some gesneriads, for example, episcias, kohlerias, smithianthas, have a scaly rhizome at the base of the stem. Others, like rechsteinerias and sinningia, have tuberous roots that act as water-storage vessels. And still others have fibrous roots.

Dark or bright light is desirable for most gesneriads. Use a loose, well-drained soil of equal parts peat moss, leaf mold, garden loam and sand. Pot plants carefully because perfect drainage is vital to successful growing. These plants require plenty of water during growth. Tepid water is best; cold water shocks the plants and causes leaves to become spotted. After flowering, most gesneriads rest, at which point you should place them in a cooler area, say 50 to 65° F., and keep the soil barely moist. At all times provide adequate moisture in the air; 30 to 40 percent will ensure healthy growth.

Hybridists have made amazing progress with gesneriads in the last few years. New and beautiful varieties are introduced frequently. Don't miss these flowers that really show:

Columnea arguta. Trailing vine, with pointed leaves and red flowers.

C. hirta. Three-inch orange blooms; vining growth.

C. microphylla. Long trailing stems with button leaves and burnt-red flowers.

C. 'Stavanger'. European hybrid, with bright red blooms.

C. 'Canary'. Cornell hybrid. Upright growth; yellow blooms.

C. 'Cornellian'. Floriferous. Orange flowers.

Episcia acajou. Silver foliage; red flowers.

E. cupreata. Hairy copper leaves; red blooms. Many forms.

E. lilacina. Bronze leaves; blue flowers.

E. 'Yellow Topaz.' Green foliage; yellow flowers.

Kohleria amabilis. Velvety green leaves; pink flowers with purple dots.

K. allenii. Hairy leaves; red-and-yellow flowers.

K. bogotensis. Speckled leaves; red-and-yellow blooms.

K. eriantha. Bright red tubular flowers.

K. hirsuta. Hairy foliage; red blooms with pale throat.

Rechsteineria cardinalis. Small green velvety leaves; scarlet tubular flowers.

R. leucotricha. Large leaves covered with silver hairs; coral blooms.

R. macropoda. Bright green leaves; small red flowers.

Sinningia 'Buell's Blue Slipper'. Velvety foliage; blue flowers.

S. 'Defiance'. Large leaves; dark crimson flowers with waxy edges.

S. 'Emperor Frederick'. Upright, dark ruby-red blooms bordered with white.

S. 'Emperor William'. Large leaves; violet blue flowers with white border.

S. 'Pink Slipper'. Light green leaves; rosy pink flowers with dark centers.

S. 'Switzerland'. Soft leaves; scarlet flowers edged white.

Smithiantha cinnabarina. Nodding, scarlet red flowers.

S. multiflora. Soft hairy plant with white blooms.

S. zebrina. Leaves covered with silky hairs; red flowers.

S. 'Golden King'. Golden yellow.

S. 'Orange King'. Orange-red.

S. 'Rose Queen'. Rose-pink.

Streptocarpus rexii. Pale blue flowers; many forms with pink, blue, white, or purple blooms.

S. saxorum. Dark green leaves; white-and-lavender flowers.

Orchids

No house-plant book is complete without orchids. These tough adaptable plants do grow and
bloom indoors, and with no more care—perhaps
less—than most house plants. Most orchids have
pseudobulbs, so if you forget to water them a few
days they still survive. Generally, orchids are of
two kinds: terrestrial (earth growing) and epiphytic
(airborne). The terrestrials grow in soil like most
other plants. The epiphytes cling to tree branches;
however, they aren't parasites and don't harm
their host.

It's best to use a special flowerpot with slots for
most orchids; the openings permit circulation of
air around the roots. (These pots are sold at orchid
nurseries.) You'll also need osmunda fiber, a
material derived from the root system of various
ferns, or a supply of fir bark, the chopped bark of
evergreens. Use either material by itself for the
epiphytes. For the terrestrials, combine one part
humus, one part leaf mold, and one part chopped
osmunda.

Pot orchids as you would any other house plant.
Provide adequate drainage material, leave space
on top for watering, and be sure the size of the
plant is in keeping with the size of the pot. Use
tepid (60 to 70° F.) water. I can't give specific rules
for watering orchids; each one must be treated
individually, and like all things with experience, the

knack of watering is learned. Or better yet, buy *Growing Orchids at Your Windows* (Hawthorn, 1973), by yours truly.

When winter heat fluctuates, so must your watering schedule. The artificial heat dries out the air, so the plants need more water. The size of the pot also affects the amount: Small pots dry out quickly, larger pots slowly.

Average room temperatures, 65 to 75° F., nicely accommodate most orchids. At night set the thermostat lower, to 50 to 60° F.; plants at your windows, like those in nature, benefit from a drop in temperature of about 10 to 15 degrees.

Most orchids don't require high humidity; 30 to 40 percent is fine. At night, along with lower temperatures, provide lower humidity. Orchids need some light, but most don't want scorching sun. The easy-to-grow kinds we're discussing here will do fine at a west, east, or even a north window. Plants must have bottom ventilation, so set them on strips of wood over clay saucers. Remember that orchids are basically air plants.

The cost of orchids ranges from five to fifteen dollars for mature specimens. There are dozens of suppliers throughout the country (see list in back of book).

Aerides odoratum. Fragrant straplike leaves; pendant scapes of white-and-pink flowers. Usually spring flowering.

Aspasia epidendroides. Grassy, paper-thin foliage; greenish-brown flowers on erect stalks. Summer and spring flowering.

Bletia purpurea. Grasslike foliage; small lavender flowers. Spring flowering.

Brassavola nodosa. Five-inch succulent green leaves; large white fragrant blooms.

Calanthe vestita. Christmas blooming; wands of red-and-white flowers.

Cattleya skinneri. Light green leathery foliage; large lavender flowers. Summer blooming.

Coelogyne flaccida. Dark green foliage; pendant coffee-colored flowers.

C. ochracea. A charmer, with grassy leaves and spring orange-and-white flowers.

Cycnoches chlorochilon. Large plant, with 7-inch chartreuse flowers shaped like a swan's neck.

Cypripedium insigne. Erect stalks of greenish blooms, typical lady-slipper type. Winter flowering.

Dendrobium jamesianum. Small plant, with large white flowers that stay fresh for months.

D. nobile hybrids. Cane-type growth, many varieties; flowers usually white, pink, and purple. Winter to spring bloom.

Epidendrum atropurpureum. Large plant, with single leathery leaves and wands of purple-and-pink blooms. Spring.

E. nemorale. Delicate flowers of lavender, many to a stem. May and June blooming.

Laelia pumila. Small plant, with pink flowers. Summer or fall blooming.

Lycaste aromatica. Medium-sized plant, with grasslike leaves and golden yellow fragrant flowers. October/November bloom.

Miltonia candida. Reddish-brown flowers with white lips in autumn.

M. spectabilis. Large rose-colored flowers with purple lips in summer.

Odontoglossum grande. Seven-inch flowers of yellow and brown; blooms in late fall.

Oncidium ampliatum. Spring flowering, with hundreds of small yellow-and-brown flowers.

O. wentworthianum. Large plant, to 40 inches. Small yellow-and-brown flowers, many to a scape, at various times of the year.

Phalaenopsis amabilis. Large plant, with broad spatula-shaped leaves and long stems of open-faced white flowers.

Renanthera imschootiana. Brilliant red flowers. Summer blooming.

Rodriguezia decora. Small plant, with white flowers spotted red. Summer blooming.

Stanhopea oculata. Broad dark green leaves; pendant scapes of lemon-yellow flowers in late summer. Grow in basket.

Trichopilia elegans. Small- to medium-sized white flowers in spring or summer.

T. tortilis. Unusual whitish-pink, corkscrew-shaped flower. Spring and summer flowering.

Vanda caerulea. Medium-sized plant. Pale blue blooms in autumn or winter.

Epiphyllums (orchid cactus)

The genus epiphyllum, more commonly known as orchid cactus, is outstanding. Native to Mexico, the West Indies, Central and South America, these plants have about twenty species that are prized for their large flowers. However, it's the thousands of hybrids that steal the show; crossed with hylocereus and selenicereus, they produce flowers of incredible size and beauty. It would seem that such beauty would be difficult to have at home, but epiphyllums are easy to grow and make ideal house plants. Most have scalloped, flat, branchy growth, and the flowers are borne on the sides of the stems.

It's important to remember that although these are cacti they grow in tropical dark forests on trees. Basically they're trailing plants, although they can be grown upright. Most epiphyllum species are large awkward plants, and their beauty and popularity have prompted growers to develop more compact plants with flowers as attractive as their larger cousins. They come in almost every color and are incredibly free flowering. None grow more than 36 inches, and many are about 24 inches, perfect for the indoor garden.

Give these plants a porous soil mixture of one-half leaf mold with equal parts of coarse gravel and garden loam. Use small pots because the root system is scanty. Bright light and average home temperatures, 72° F. by day, 62° F. at night, suit most of the plants. Provide 30 to 50 percent humidity, and allow the soil to dry out completely between waterings; epiphyllum roots must not be surrounded by soggy soil. Repot the plants only when absolutely necessary; it's much better to top-dress them because they resent any root disturbance. Don't feed plants. Peak flowering is May and June. With careful selection, a dozen plants give color at the window for about two months. Try the following varieties (listed by color):

Red

'Bacchus'	'Greek God'
'Cardinal'	'Holiday'
'Fireside'	'Imp'

Purple and Orchid

'Adventure'	'Gertrude W. Beahm'
'Arctic Waters'	'Harmony'
'Ceylon'	'Jungle Night'

White, Cream, and Yellow

'Albino'
'Baby Doll'
'Champagne'

'Fanciful'
'Halo'
'Polar Bear'

Light Pink, Dark Pink

'Angel Serenade'
'Fairy Queen'
'Flower Song'

'Princess Betty'
'Carnation'
'Cuthbert'

Orange

'Cherokee Chief'
'Cup of Gold'
'Keepsake'

'Rosa Rita'
'Sunland'
'Susquehanna'

For the Adventurer

Here are a few afterthoughts and sometimes these thoughts are better than planned ones. These are plants from Chapter 2 that need some sun. For example, hibiscus. This is a stellar flowering plant that needs buckets of water; most varieties start blooming in late fall when color is especially desirable in dark apartments. *Dipladenia amoena,* the Mexican love vine, is for summer cheer. It likes to be grown in a hanging planter and it too needs plenty of water to coax the bounty of pink flowers in summer. Another goodie!

Not to be forgotten is my favorite: *Clerodendrum thomsoniae,* the glory bower. This beauty is tough to get going, but once established bears two crops of dramatic red-and-white flowers. Certainly worth a college try. And while you are trying, sample the ginger plant known as hedychium—a lovely sight in bloom. *Heliconia aurantiaca,* which is a member of the banana family, bears bird-of-paradise-type flowers; it did for me in a dim Chicago apartment, and last but not least, by all means grow some garden-type impatiens for bright red color. They can and do bloom indoors! Ask for dwarf types. Real gems.

8 Ferns for Beauty

There's something about ferns that's universally pleasing. They're lush, green, and delicate, and, quite frankly, you'll either be able to grow them or not. My mother grew ferns with abandon in dark corners, anywhere and everywhere, and they grew like sweet potatoes. I'm death to ferns, but take your chances, and let's hope you're not like me when it comes to ferns. Ferns have been around since prehistoric times and have an intense desire to live, so green your dark corners with filmy fronds of loveliness for one and all.

The trouble with ferns is that there are so many (about 6,000 species), and all too often they're sold under incorrect names. Some ferns are epiphytes and grow in treetops; some climb trees; and others—the ones for us—like moist, dark places.

How to Care for Ferns

Light, Air, and Humidity

In a north location ferns are protected from the harmful direct midday sun, yet they receive whatever light they need. Most ferns thrive at 70 to 80° F. during the day, with a gradual decrease in temperature to 55 to 60° F. at night. You should give your ferns sufficient ventilation, but beware of drafts because they're extremely injurious to plants. You'll have to see that they get good humidity, so grow a few ferns together, or set single plants in gravel pans filled with water; that is, the gravel should be moist, but the pot should never be sitting in water.

Soil and Repotting

Grow ferns in a loose potting soil. Add some osmunda (available from suppliers) to keep the mix porous. A satisfactory soil consists of one part leaf mold, one part fibrous peat, and one part sand. Clay pots are the best containers because the clay lets moisture evaporate gradually from within the pot's walls. This helps ferns because, as mentioned, they like their roots cool and moist. Plastic pots don't keep moisture within their walls (plastic is nonporous).

Repot plants only when absolutely necessary. Most ferns like to be potbound, and a mature plant in a 12-inch pot can go three years without repotting. (Smaller plants need more frequent repotting.)

You can repot ferns at any time of the year, but February and March are the best months because warm weather, which encourages development and growth, is on the way. Use clean, dry pots. Soak new and old ones in water for a few hours; unsoaked pots absorb a lot of water and rob the freshly potted plant of moisture. Fern roots grasp the inside of the pot walls, so if you pull them loose they are injured. Rap the container sharply against a table edge, and tease the plant out. If this doesn't work, break the container with a hammer (most clay pots are inexpensive). If you're dealing with a large fern and don't want to bruise it, turn it upside down while it's still in its pot and wrap the plant in a large towel or in newspaper to protect the fronds and make repotting easier.

Now crumble away old soil and trim dead (brown) roots slightly. Put the fern in a container on a generous bed of crushed gravel; add soil in and around the crown of the plant. Push down slightly (but not hard) to firm the soil. *Don't* jam the plant into the pot; use a pot large enough to last for two years' growth (but not so large that the plant will look ungainly). A plant from a 6-inch pot should go into an 8-inch container, one in a 10-inch container should go into a 12-inch pot, and so on. Water the soil thoroughly several times to really soak it and to eliminate all air pockets. Now isolate the plant; place it in a bright place and water it moderately for a few weeks. It's then ready for its permanent place in the room.

Watering and Feeding

Various conditions determine when you should water ferns: pot size (large pots dry out slower than small ones), individual growing conditions, the weather, and the plant itself. Plants grow very slowly in cloudy, cool weather, and overwatering won't force them into growth—it will kill them! Too much water also can cause a fern to die if growing conditions lack humidity. Water large plants twice a week in spring and summer and once a week or every ten days in fall and winter (when most ferns rest).

When you water, soak the plant and then allow it to dry out a bit before watering it again. Once a month leach the plant to get rid of harmful salts. (Leaching is described in Chapter 4.) *Never* use icy cold water for ferns because it will harm foliage; let a bucket of water stand overnight, and then water in the morning. Try not to get moisture on the fronds or a fungus may develop on the foliage. Keep tops of plants dry.

Finally, don't forget that there's no cure for ferns once roots dry out and fronds droop. Watering dry roots doesn't perk up the foliage as it does with many other plants.

Avoid excessive feeding; most ferns react adversely to any feeding (for example, several plants I grow develop brown leaves even with moderate feeding, but I do give weak solutions of fish emulsion, which seem very satisfactory).

Move plants a quarter turn every month or so to ensure the beautiful symmetry of the fern (a lopsided plant isn't handsome). Allow enough space between plants or between plant and wall so fronds don't come in contact with anything. This will prevent ugly bruises on your delicate fern.

The Best Ferns

Nephrolepis (Boston fern)

This is the most popular fern but ironically the most difficult to keep in good greenness. But it can succeed even in a dark corner if you do these two little things: Soak it thoroughly in water in your bathtub once a week to the rim of the pot, and mist it frequently. If you don't have a bathtub, use the sink, or take it in the shower with you. Don't feed; don't pamper—just let it be, or, best yet, grow it on an inverted pot or some kind of pedestal because fronds eventually droop and become bruised if hit. Do keep the fern in somewhat cool conditions, about 55° F. at night and not much higher during the day if you can help it. And, as mentioned in Chapter 4, avoid 'Fluffy Ruffles' and 'Rooseveltii' varieties because they are temperamental.

Davallias

Here's a group of lovely epiphytic ferns that shouldn't be missed. Mine has grown in a dark corner of the bathroom for years; it's a mass of delicate filmy fronds, lovely to behold in morning or anytime. These green tapestries have furry rhizomes that like to crawl over the soil mix. Let them crawl; don't bury them or you bury the plant too. Let the roots lie scandent on the soil, and keep the plant somewhat moist and dark. Although davallias are tropical plants, I find they just love my unheated bathroom (about 55° F.). Use a loose potting mix of equal parts soil and chopped osmunda.

There are many davallias, and they're all good; here's a partial listing:

D. bullata mariesii. Very filmy and delicate looking.

D. canariensis. Hardy foliage and somewhat more robust.

D. pentaphylla. The true hare's foot fern; thick fronds and lovely. *Note:* Also sold as a davallia, *Polypodium aureum* (false hare's foot fern) is a nuisance; avoid it.

Asplenium

There are many species in this group but most are trouble. However, *A. nidus,* the bird's-nest fern, is quite at home in a shady corner. Unlike most ferns with filmy fronds this one has broad leaves in a rosette growth habit. Keep the soil evenly moist and provide good humidity for this fern. This is not a spectacular plant but it certainly is an easy one to grow and a mature specimen is handsome on table or desk.

Pellaea (button-fern)

These ferns with heart-shaped segments are somewhat different in appearance than most ferns since they lack conventional fronds. The tiny button-shaped leaves are quite handsome and the plant grows low and full so it makes a nice decorator accent. Button-ferns do have one strict requirement though: They must have excellent drainage because a soggy soil will kill them quickly. The popular species and one I suggest is *P. rotundifolia;* when small, leaves are somewhat tiny, but as the plants mature leaves become full and lush. Grow in a bright or shady place.

Pteris (brake-ferns)

Pteris (pronounced *terrace*) ferns are a large group of small plants with feathery growth. Some recent hybrids are variegated and make dramatic plants. Plants will want some bright light in winter but the rest of the year do just fine in shade. Keep soil evenly moist and as with most ferns, provide adequate humidity (about 50 percent). Under good conditions pteris ferns are rapid growers, so try one if you are an impatient gardener (and who isn't?).

Woodwardia (chain-fern)

Not often seen, woodwardias make good indoor plants although they do grow rather large. As hanging subjects they are fine though, and can add great color to a room. Foliage is leathery and somewhat stiff, dark green rather than the light green color of most ferns. Plants will need a good soaking in the sink once a month, but otherwise require little attention. Give them a nice shady nook and keep soil evenly moist. Good one to try if you are tired of the conventional Boston fern.

9 Bulbs for Drama

If you think bulbs are strictly for outdoors, think again, my friend. Lovely flowering bulbs can brighten any dark corner and bring a kaleidoscope of colorful blooms to your jaded eyes. Look and enjoy. There's the fiery red blossoms of amaryllis, the orange crowns of flowers of clivia, and the blue beauty of scilla, to mention only a few. And with bulbs the work is done for you because that funny looking onionlike tuber already has its own food; all it needs is a little light and some water to get it moving.

How to Care for Bulbous Plants

Buy top-quality bulbs; this makes a difference. Don't look for bargains. Old bulbs are more apt to chase you back into the dark corner. Some bulbs will be precooled (forced bulbs, as they're called in the catalogs); these are the ones you want for indoors.

Bulbs such as common crocus and narcissus, which need a two-month dark period, are ideal. Plant them in gravel or soil, and then move them to a bright light only when you see tips' growth. Hyacinths too do best in dim light, even when started. Few bulbs should be exposed to full sun, which we assume you don't have anyway, so bulbs are your light in the darkness.

The Best Bulbs

Hyacinth

A glass jar, some water, and charcoal chips— your hyacinth is now ready for planting, or rather, placing. Place the bulb in the jar so the water is just touching the base of the bulb. Put the jar in a cool, dark place, about 55° F., and leave it for eight to twelve weeks. An out-of-the-way corner (where there's little light, natural or artificial), under a shelf, in the bathroom, or any place where it isn't bright is fine. When the bulb starts pushing out, bring it into filtered light and warmer temperatures to bring forth its crown of flowers.

French Roman hyacinths are available pre-cooled from many sources. Plant in early October for Christmas, or in December for February grandeur.

Amazon lily *(Eucharis grandiflora)*

The grandiflora end of the name suits this magnificent flowering plant: It bears dazzling 2-inch white flowers, sweet and fragrant for Christmas, or in midsummer. The dark green leaves are handsome and straplike, in a rosette form (never cut the leaves), and flowers top 24-inch stems with three or six to a cluster. This one needs house-plant soil and 75° F. by day, 65° F. by night. Even in a dim corner the Amazon lily will bear its blossoms. After the plant blooms, reduce water gradually and move it to a very dark, cool place to rest a bit. In six or eight weeks start the cycle again. Let plants become potbound rather than starting new bulbs or dividing each year. This lovely bulb can grow into a mammoth pot plant. I had one in a 10-inch pot; including foliage and flowers, it measured 18 inches across.

Amaryllis

The Dutch growers offer these bulbs, which can be planted from November on, available in an array of colors—red, salmon, white, or pink—or, if you're very fussy, ask for the many fine named varieties. Plant the bulbs when you get them; generally most bloom in winter, with strong straplike leaves *after* the magnificent huge flowers with three or four broad, flat-faced blooms. Use clean, deep pots because amaryllis roots go deep, and select pots that allow a 1-inch margin around the bulb. Use a commercial soil mix and moisten it well. Leave bulbs in a dark place until the flowering stalk appears, and then move it into light. Heat will make the bulbs come along faster.

After blooms fade, cut away the flower stalk and water less but enough to keep leaves growing to store up energy in the bulb for next year's flowers. When growth is complete, dry out bulbs and store them in a dark place for several months, with just scant watering.

Aztec lily (Sprekelia)

If you've always wanted a lily in your house, here's your chance to have one with vivid red flowers to 6 inches, no less. Generally flowers appear in early spring. Plant this way: Use one bulb to a pot, with the shoulders exposed and a 1-inch margin around the bulb to edge of container. Use an all-purpose soil mixture and water thoroughly. Keep growing in a somewhat warm (75° F.), shady (not sunny) place. If the gods are with you, flower stalks will start pushing through in January or so, at which time you can put the plant into bright light. New bulbs must be started every year.

Veltheimia

This is a beautiful plant that bears clusters of rose-and-green flowerets on a 20-inch stem. Even without flowers the rich, dark green leaves are handsome, and best of all, blooms appear in January or February, when color is so welcome indoors. Pot the bulb when you get it in all-purpose soil. Fit it closely in the pot, with about a 1-inch margin of soil around the bulb and with the shoulders exposed. Water, but not too much, and keep it rather cool in a bright place. When it starts growing, increase moisture, and about every third week give it a weak solution of any old plant food. Flowers are unusual and well worth your time.

Kafir-lily *(Clivia miniata)*

This aristocrat of the amaryllis family will glow with color in any dark corner. With handsome green straplike leaves and clusters of vivid orange flowers, I recommend this plant to any beginner. In early spring when clivia blooms, he will feel like a proud parent. Naturally growing in shady places, this flowering gem is easy to grow indoors but with a few idiosyncrasies. Keep it in shade and the soil moist, let it dry out somewhat after flowering (for about a month or more) but do not let it get bone dry. And last but not least, to have a blooming clivia with you, keep it potbound. That is, repot only when necessary (about every third year), but do top-dress the soil with fresh soil every year. Many fine hybrids are available.

Blood-lily (Haemanthus)

Don't let the name scare you because this is a splendid indoor plant that has luxuriant fleshy leaves and hundreds of tiny flowers in a sphere. Most unique, pot the blood-lily with tip protruding in a 5- to 7-inch container of soil. Give plants plenty of water in summer, not so much in winter when a rest of four to six weeks is in order. *H. coccineus* is the most popular species and flowers are blood-red in color. *H. katherinae* is also fine with salmon-red blooms.

While these are spectacular plants, I do want to mention that they are not as easy to grow as most plants in this section but certainly are worth the effort. And they will also need somewhat more light than most plants we have discussed. But if you have some mad money, do give haemanthus a try.

Pineapple-lily (Eucomis)

I have seen this plant appearing more and more at flower shows and in shops so thought I would mention it. Eucomis has shiny green foliage and handsome crowns of tiny flowers in summer. Because the plant does bloom in bright light (direct sun not necessary), it is a fine subject for indoor growing where some color is needed. Like the other lilies mentioned here, eucomis too needs a somewhat dry rest in winter with just sparse watering. Another good one!

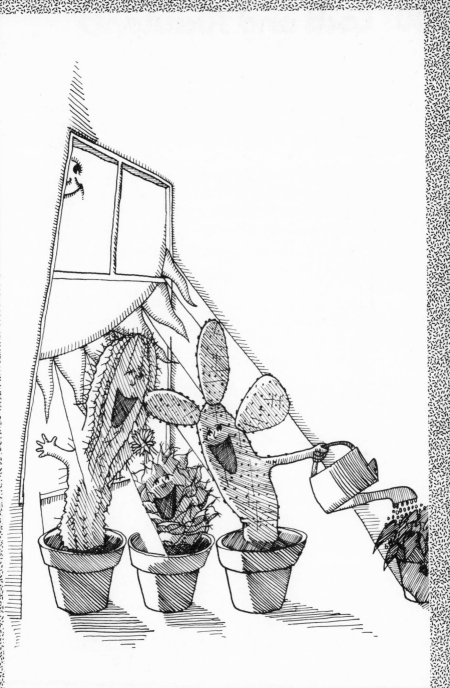

10 Cacti and Succulents

If someone tells you cacti and succulents need sun, sun, sun, tell them they're wrong, wrong, wrong. I think these satisfying indoor plants could grow in a closet if necessary—not all, but the ones we'll mention here. I have six or seven cacti that are large and in dim corners, and yet they grow six inches a year, hardly a reluctant plant. The trick is to water very sparingly and to start with a good-sized plant, three or four feet tall. I water my plants only once a month; the secret is that the soil mix has equal parts of soil and gravel chips or stones. Drainage must be perfect, and gravel or stones will do it and save you from getting addlebrained about dying cacti. Always remember that cacti store water, so that's the reason for this seemingly cruel treatment.

How to Care for Cacti

Soil

Cacti don't grow in pure sand as most people think. Just like other plants they need a good soil mix with the right nutrients. Which soil mixture you choose among the many available depends upon the size and type of plant you're growing. Most cacti are desert dwellers, but some, like the Christmas cactus, are native to the rain forests and thus need a different type of soil.

Use a mix of equal parts of garden loam and small pebbles for most cacti. For jungle cacti, e.g., rhipsalis, schlumbergera and zygocactus, use a mixture of one part shredded tree bark or osmunda (sold at nurseries) and one part garden loam. Mix the ingredients *thoroughly,* making sure the soil has a friable texture so it drains water, yet retains moisture for plant roots.

Prepared soil sold by nurseries contains all the necessary nutrients for plant growth, although I prefer to add some pebbles. This soil is sterilized, which means you rarely have to worry about weeds or bacterial diseases starting. The packaged soil prepared especially for cacti is also satisfactory, but stay away from mixes specifically marked for African violets or house plants because they're generally too heavy and dense for good cacti growth.

Soilless mixes or peat mixes (also available at nurseries) are lightweight and good for some plants but aren't suitable for cacti because they contain no nutrients; this means that you have to carefully feed your cacti, which is too time consuming.

Light and Temperature

Cacti generally need good light, at least some sun a few hours a day, to really thrive. However, even in lesser situations they'll still survive, although they won't grow rapidly. Don't expect every cacti to bloom unless they are in a very sunny location. Select zygocactus, rhipsalis, lobivias, parodias, rebutias and epiphyllums. They not only produce flowers but can, if they have to, bloom in lower light levels. Turn plants occasionally (unless they're in bud) so light evenly reaches all parts of the plant; otherwise plants will lean toward the light, and who wants a lopsided cactus?

Most cacti are flexible as to temperatures, tolerating from 55 to 90° F. without harm, although 75° F. by day and 65° F. at night is ideal. Most cacti rest in winter and need less warmth, so lower temperatures of 65° F. by day and 55° F. by night are very beneficial.

Watering

Watering cacti depends upon the plant itself, the container and the soil. Generally water desert cacti in large containers (over 14 inches) twice a week through spring and summer, once a week in fall, and once a month in winter. (Keep jungle cacti moist all year.) You can water smaller plants in smaller containers somewhat but not much more. A good rule is: When you see plants in active growth (fresh green shoots), water the plant. But when plants are resting, don't try to force them into growth; it won't work, and you'll lose the plant from overwatering. Always use tepid water because cold water shocks plants. And if possible, water in the morning so plants can dry out somewhat before evening. As mentioned, clay pots dry out faster than plastic or glazed ones, and plants in dry sunny locations need more water than those in only bright light. However, when in doubt, *don't water!*

Feeding

Don't think that all plants require feeding to make them grow. This will make the chemical manufacturers' profits grow but not the plant. This especially applies to cacti. The only exceptions are specimen plants—those that have been in very large pots for years—because soil has been depleted of nutrients. Supplemental feeding is necessary with specimen plants for continued growth and vigor. Fertilize these plants once a month during the growing season with a weak solution of a fertilizer such as 5–10–10.

Most cacti at one time of the year (usually winter) need a short rest to regain strength for another period of growth. (Exceptions are the shade-loving jungle cacti like epiphyllums, Christmas and Easter cacti, and rhipsalis. These plants must be regularly watered all year long.) This hiatus in activity is essential to their well-being and is a natural part of their life cycle. In winter, try to give plants somewhat cooler temperatures (about 55° F.), and water soil just enough so it doesn't become caked. Don't feed or try to force plants into growth; the result will be abnormal growth and a possible loss of flowers in summer. The rest period generally lasts for about one month to six weeks; the plant will tell you when it's ready for more water and warmer temperatures: You'll see fresh growth and the plant will, usually, assume a more perky look.

The Best Plants

Cacti

Cephalocerous palmeri (wooly torch). This is generally a column-shaped plant, with short blue-green spines and tufts of white wooly hairs completely covering it. More of an oddity than a beauty, it has a unique look and does well under adverse conditions.

Chamaecereus silverstrii (peanut cactus). A fine branching cacti, with clusters of short, spiny, green branches. Even small plants make a nice showing, and the red flowers on this one will make you love it. It will withstand a six- or nine-month period in dark corners, but in summer give it some bright light. Keep almost dry during the winter, with slightly cool temperatures (60° F.).

Echinocactus grusonii (golden barrel). A truly beautiful plant, the golden barrel is a symmetrical globe covered with sharp golden yellow spines; large plants (about 8 inches in diameter) are delightful decorative accents. These plants are murderous to handle, but once planted, the golden barrel can remain in its pot for four or five years. It grows slowly and takes little light. Mine (now seven years old) has never really seen the light of day. It resides in a dark north corner and loves it!

E. baileyi. Another good echinocactus, as easy to grow as the golden barrel, is this column-shaped cactus with white spines which adds a cheerful note indoors. The flowers are bright yellow and large. It needs somewhat more light than most cacti, but mine has done well at a west window with little sun. Echinocactus offers easy gardening for the amateur and almost grows on its own.

Mammillaria bocasana (powder-puff cactus). I've never been overly fond of this plant, yet it remains attractive and healthy in the dining room with little help from me—stubborn, I guess. It has clustering growth, hooked central spines covered with white hair, and occasionally, in defiance of me, bears small pretty yellow flowers. A robust plant that out of fairness I must recommend.

Notocactus haselbergii (scarlet ball). This globe-shaped cactus is covered with soft white spines, and like most notocactus is an excellent blooming plant that will bear flowers, unlike many cacti that won't indoors. The plants are especially rewarding because, again, like most of my cacti, they require little light. Mine resides in the kitchen at a north window with little care.

Opuntia basilaris (beaver tail). This group of overrated cacti never really look attractive and have a tendency to grow straggly after a time. They have blue-green pads, one growing on top of the other, and seem to belong in the desert rather than in a house. Still, because they're well known they're included here, and I must admit that they grow easily with little care.

Parodia. These small but pretty cacti should be in everyone's house. They're charming, do bloom indoors, and the flowers are pretty and well worth the space the plant takes. They're a nice touch of color year 'round, and I wouldn't be without them. Species include *P. aureispina* (Tom Thumb cactus) and *P. sanguiniflora*.

Rebutia minuscula (red crown cactus). This small, fine, globe-shaped plant has brilliant red flowers about 2 inches across. Such beauty is worth everyone's attention, and rebutias grow easily indoors. Try to give them some bright light to coax flowers, but even in a dark place the plants without blooms will be handsome.

How to Care for Succulents

Succulents are plants with fleshy leaves and, like cacti, can store water in case you forget them. In addition, while most succulents need good light, there are many that make fine indoor plants where light is less than enviable. Because there are so many succulent plants (they appear in many plant families) it is impossible to give specific care, but some general information on how to keep them healthy is included here.

Use the same soil mix you have for cacti for your succulent plants and in general keep plants in small pots. Many succulents seem to grow better when they are somewhat potbound. Agaves and crassulas are prime examples.

While good bright light will bring better color and growth to succulents, a great many can fare well even in shade if necessary. However, unlike cacti, which may bloom in shady places, most succulents will not grow flowers, so be content with the lovely foliage.

Water plants somewhat heavily in summer but the rest of the year keep soil just evenly moist. With some succulents (depending on the genus) you will have to give plants a rest in winter and keep soil just barely moist and at lower temperatures (10 degrees lower) than during the growing season. Again, as in cacti culture, use tepid water for plants and try not to get too much water on foliage as staining can result. If plants are showing new growth (generally in spring or fall) it is fine to give them adequate water, but otherwise keep them on the dry side.

With succulents you can feed them somewhat more than cacti but never too much. In spring and summer use a 10–10–5 plant food once a month and not at all the rest of the year. Remember that plants in shady places simply cannot assimilate plant food as readily as those in sunny places, so feed accordingly.

Occasionally, insects might attack succulent plants (See Chapter 12) but don't panic. A systemic insecticide applied in granular form to the soil and then watered will eliminate most, but not all, insects. The best preventative against insect attack (as with all plants) is close observation and catching trouble before it starts. It's easy to eliminate a few aphids or pick off a small colony of scale with a toothpick, but massive attacks (which should not happen indoors) will call for more drastic measures. Be smart—look, see, and enjoy your plants, but at the same time watch out for those crawling, creepy things.

Succulents

Agave victoriae reginae. Want to be the envy of the neighborhood? Grow this agave; it's an impressive plant with narrow olive-green leaves in a compact rosette. It looks more like a sculpture than a plant, and at five or ten dollars a plant serves its purpose well. Don't get water on its leaves or water it too much because it likes a somewhat dry existence throughout its life. My plant finally grew so big across that I took it from its 10-inch pot and planted it outdoors, which wasn't a wise decision because although our temperatures are not supposed to drop below 40° F., they did. After two nights at 31 degrees, the agave was mush!

Aloe nobilis. This is a rather ugly plant, but it is easy to grow in dim light so is included here. My main complaint about aloes is that the clustered rosette growth is never symmetrical or overly attractive. Otherwise they're amenable plants that can withstand abuse.

Crassula argentea (jade plant). Here's my candidate for a plant that can take darkness and still be beautiful. It has succulent bright green round leaves edged in red, and mature species with their branching habit are impressive "trees" at home. Keep it somewhat dry, and don't baby it.

Euphorbia splendens (crown of thorns). This plant joined my collection in Illinois. It was in a 6-inch pot, a thoroughly lovely branching plant with tiny dark green leaves and thorny branches. With some clipping and trimming the crown of thorns was shaped into a thing of beauty. I kept it on a low table at a north window, where it grew lavishly. Here in California at the same exposure it doesn't do as well. Perhaps the plant is a dedicated Midwesterner, but nonetheless, it's beautiful and heartily recommended.

Euphorbia obesa (basketball plant). As different as day from night, this plant hardly resembles most euphorbias. It's a richly colored, rounded, ridged ball. More of a curiosity than a plant, it offers good color and is so easy to grow, even in dimly lighted areas, that it has my recommendation. Don't expect miracles from it though; it grows slowly.

Kalanchoe blossfeldiana. This is a superb flowering plant, with tiny red or orange blooms. *K. blossfeldiana* deserves indoor space for any garden lover. The clustering succulent dark green leaves are handsome, and if you cut off the first batch of faded flowers in winter, in spring you'll be rewarded with another crop. Quite a harvest of color from a plant that costs about five dollars. Other kalanchoes such as *K. tomentosa* (the panda plant) and *K. fedtschenkoi* seem to do just as well in nonsunny places.

Sedum. A large group of some good, some bad plants, most with small succulent rounded leaves. *S. morganianum,* the burro's tail, is a good house plant. Grow it in a basket but do try some other sedums. They seem to thrive indoors even without light, and all in all, although not spectacular, they make nice green accents.

11 Artificial Light When All Else Fails

Artificial light (fluorescent and incandescent) has been a boon to the home gardener and rightly so. A single incandescent lamp or a pair of 20-watt fluorescent lamps can nurse a plant back to health in a dim corner. If this seems an exaggeration, put a plant under your favorite reading lamp. If the light is on a reasonable time (say four or five hours), you'll notice within a week that the plant has perked up; leaves will seem greener, stems strong.

Fluorescent light has been compared to sunlight, but this is somewhat an exaggerated claim. However, it does emit essential blue rays that make foliage plants grow well. Incandescent light is rich in red and far-red rays, also essential to plant growth. After much experimentation by the USDA and dedicated plantsmen, it has been decided that a combination of both light sources makes a plant really give its all. This is true, and I've found it to work wonders for many but not all the house plants I've grown. Other factors such as light intensity, duration, the type of plant being grown, temperature, humidity, and ventilation must all be considered too.

At this point you're probably saying that this is all too complex for me—and perhaps you're right. The basic thing to remember is: If there's some natural light, the addition of an incandescent or fluorescent lamp will make plants grow better. It's as simple as that. And whereas lamp fixtures used to be ugly, now there are handsome ones that fit almost any room decor, for example, tray units and

table lamps. Forget the carts and elaborate mova-
ble gardens made for many plants; in most cases
you'll be concerned with only a few plants.

The cost of using artificial light is minimal, and
the results can be rewarding. The drawback is that
you might want *all* your plants under lights. This is
where you can get into trouble because then special units and devices are necessary, and before
long you end up with more equipment than plants.
So keep it simple. Your plants *and* your pocketbook will be better off.

Fluorescent Light

Fluorescent lamps include special plant-growth
kinds such as Plant Gro and Gro-Lux. These are
supposed to give balanced artificial light. Other
fluorescents—the standard types—come in a variety of lengths and intensities and qualities of light
and are designated cool white, daylight, and so
forth. I've found cool white the best for plants.

How much fluorescent light should a plant get?
This depends on the plant itself. For example, the
plants mentioned in this book for dark or shady
places will need only 10 to 15 watts per square
foot, while some flowering plants will need 25 to
30 watts per square foot. One of the best indica-
tors of whether a plant is getting enough light is
the plant. If it is growing leggy it needs more light;
if leaves are faded, you are giving the plant too
much light.

You can use either incandescent or fluorescent light to supplement natural light. In general, for this situation give plants four or five hours of artificial light. If you are growing plants only with artificial light, then most plants need about twelve to fourteen hours of light every day.

As mentioned, you can simply use an incandescent lamp for plants or you might want to buy one of the commercial fluorescent light units. There are table models for a few plants or carts for many plants. You can also make your own light setup with lamps and reflector fixtures. A simple home installation is to use a slimline fluorescent lamp installed under counters in say, the kitchen. This will accommodate several small plants away from windows.

Incandescent Light

The prime example of incandescent light is an ordinary reading lamp. I have several African violets in a bathroom where there is hardly any natural light. There is a small reconverted kerosene lamp on the shelf with a 60-watt bulb in it. I purposely leave this light on in the evening for five or six hours and these plants flourish. The combination of some natural light and incandescent works well for the plants. So a reading lamp is fine for plants but you might want to get more sophisticated, and in this case you can use some of the new incandescent grow-lamps. There are table models that can be placed almost anywhere to accommodate a few plants.

Other incandescent lamps include floodlights; these need special bullet- or canopy-type fixtures to direct the light to the plant. The heat from these can be intense and can harm a plant so keep the light source at least 3 to 4 feet from the plant. This means that generally fixtures must be in or near the ceiling. If you have a special plant in a dark corner by all means consider this setup. Yes, it is costly, but it will keep that handsome plant in good health for many years instead of only a year, say.

And if you really want to go all out you might want to try the mercury vapor lamps. These have both fluorescent lamps and incandescent elements in the same housing. There are several available; one of the easiest to use is sold under the name Fluomeric and is manufactured by the Duro-Test Corporation. Mercury vapor lamps are also available under other trade names, so check with local dealers. These lamps too, like floodlights, must be placed at least 4 to 5 feet from the plants.

In Summary

Whichever lamps you use, and this depends greatly on how many plants you have and on your pocketbook, remember that none of them are miracle workers by themselves. Plants will still need some attention and this means adequate and correct watering, ventilation, feeding and all the other things previously discussed in this book. And as you change the light conditions for plants you change their requirements. As mentioned many times previously, the more light the plant gets the more water it needs and so on. That is why this chapter has the title it has; growing plants under artificial light means somewhat more work and time on your part but when all else fails, it is the only way to keep plants alive in very dark situations.

12 Don't Worry Them to Death

If a plant doesn't grow or starts to lose vigor, most people panic and immediately rush to the nursery to buy insecticides. In most cases this is a waste of money and time because the problem may be culture rather than insects, or the plant may be resting or trying to rest. Although some plants do need constant care, the ones we talk about in this book are better off with some careful neglect. Plants have been around for ages and they have an intense desire to live. With just a little bit of help from you they'll manage fine. However, with too much help from you you can kill them.

If leaves drop or turn brown, look first to culture rather than insects before you spray. It may be that repotting to improve drainage, an increase in humidity, or simply some fresh air will bring plants back to health. (On the other hand, insecticides may have killed the plant.)

Possible Ailments

Now that you've kept your head (and your plant) by not dousing it with chemicals, sit down and rationally determine just what is wrong with a plant. Plants, like people, give clues if things are awry. For example, here are some possible plant ailments: brown or yellow leaves, leaves dropping, foliage with white rings, pale leaves or weak growth, slow growth, crumbling leaves. Insects? Not necessarily. Inspect plants carefully; most of the common insects are easily seen—mealybugs in leaf axils, aphids on stems or leaves, scale attached to stems. Even red spiders, too diminutive to be seen by the naked eye, leave a telltale web. If the problem isn't insects, follow this chart:

Brown or yellow leaves	Heat too high, too low humidity, soil too dry/wet.
Leaf drop	Temperature extremes; cold water; humidity too low.
Foliage spots	Cold water; drafts.
Pale leaves weak growth	Needs more light; heat too high; too much food.
Slow growth	Poorly drained soil; plants may be resting naturally.
Crumbling leaves	Too high heat; too low humidity.
Collapse of plant	Drafts; fluctuating temperatures.

Pests and Diseases

If culture is good and plants still fail, then a nefarious insect or, more rarely, bacteria may be at work. As mentioned, most insects are recognizable; the problem isn't so much finding the insect as *which* insect. Different insects need different remedies, and there's no one cure-all. So the first step is to know the common insects and what they look like. At first you might say this is beyond your grasp; you're growing plants, not insects, and don't want to be bothered. That's a pessimistic approach—there's little trouble in knowing the insects, and after a while they're quite interesting. Consider them a form of life you're not familiar with (and don't want to be familiar with), but if you love your plants you will persevere. Here's a list of insects:

Mealybugs	White cottony clusters in stem and leaf.
Thrips	Almost invisible yellow, brown, or black sucking insects.
Aphids	Green, black, or red oval varmints about 1/16 inch long.
Mites	Tiny, tiny devils (these you can't see).
White flies	Swarm and look like very small mosquitos.
Red spider	Tough to see but telltale webs exist.
Scale	Ovoid in shape, with hard or soft shells, about 1/8 inch long.
Slugs or snails	No mistaking these.

Now that you've the list of offenders, what to do? Here are some general rules (specific ones come later). If the attack is light, try a vigorous spray of soapy water (not a detergent) followed by a clear rinsing. To eliminate aphids, thoroughly wash the plant at the sink, or with a small brush douse aphids with a solution of a tablespoon of alcohol dissolved in a quart of soapy water. A mixture of soap and water deters red spiders, and mealybugs wither from an alcohol dab. Scale is somewhat more difficult to eliminate, but soak old cigarette tobacco in water a few days and then apply it with a toothbrush to get rid of these pests. Cut potatoes in half to lure snails and slugs to where you can destroy them. And pour hot water over the soil of plants to chase springtails into the saucer; then wash them away.

These rules are easy ways out without resorting to chemicals, but if pests persist, it's time to use some insecticides (but with a judicious hand). All-purpose aerosols are one answer, and they will eliminate some, but not all, insects. Read the can to determine what the spray will kill. The advantage of the aerosol is that you don't have to mix anything.

If you don't use an aerosol, buy malathion (which smells awful), and mix it with water as prescribed on the package. Better yet, try nicotine sulfate (not as strong or odoriferous); follow package directions. You'll need Dimite or Kelthane for mites. That's it; don't bother with any other poisons in the house. Do keep these out of the reach of children and pets, and don't ever use them in a kitchen area.

One more note (and a good one): systemics. These are granular insecticides you apply to the soil and then water. These chemicals protect plants from the majority of sucking and chewing insects for six to eight weeks. The insecticide is drawn up by roots into sap streams, thus making it toxic.

Now a few notes about plant diseases, which quite frankly are rare, but if I don't cover them, I'll hear about it. Here are the diseases that might affect some plants:

Mildew	Leaves or soil coated white	Spray with Karathane or Phaltan.
Botrytis blight	Gray mold on leaves	Spray with Zineb.
Virus disease	Leaves or stems streaked, circled, or pitted	Destroy plant

Abandonment When Necessary

This practice seems cruel, yet it's sometimes the most prudent way to deal with virus-infected or other plants that are beyond saving. Better this than have all the plants in your home get ill. If you can't bear to throw out your green gems, try isolating plants without water for a while to see if you can pull them through.

13 Grow Your Own

I've said it many times in plant books, and I'll say it again here because it's universally true: Everyone likes something for nothing, and with plants you can get something for nothing. A cutting from a plant, a piece of it, or a leaf can in a few months give you another plant with little trouble. Further cuttings give you plants in quick time compared to seed sowing, which takes time (although seed sowing is a very cheap propagation method).

Always remember that house plants won't last a lifetime, especially if they're grown in somewhat dark places, so it makes good sense and is good insurance to snip cuttings from your plants and keep them growing to replace any plants you may lose.

Cuttings

You can take a cutting from a plant, plunk it in a jar of water, wait until it forms roots, and then pot it. This is fine for some plants, but the majority require a little more time and effort. The cuttings must be rooted in a growing medium and given some extra care until they're ready for little pots.

To take a cutting, remove 3 to 4 inches from the tip of a stem; that's all there is to it. Do this in spring or early summer, which is the plant's natural growth time. Forget doing it in fall and winter—it just won't work well. When you have your cutting, leave the tip leaves but discard the rest. As mentioned, you can try just plunking the cutting in water, but a better method is to use a discarded household container such as a frozen-roll container, a cottage-cheese carton, or, if fancy, a glass dish. And, of course, you can always use a standard pot for the cutting. Be sure that whatever it is, it has drainage holes. Put 3 to 4 inches of vermiculite (sold at suppliers) or a sand mixture into the container. Dip the newly cut stem end in rooting hormone, and then put it in the growing medium. Place the cuttings so there's space between them, and cover the cuttings with a Baggie on sticks. Make a tent so humidity is trapped within the housing to nourish the new seedlings.

Water the medium, but don't drench it. Place the cuttings in a warm (75° F.), dark place. (The top of the refrigerator has always been my favorite place for cuttings.) In a few weeks remove the plastic, pull up a cutting, and see if roots have formed. If you've been successful, now transfer the new plant to a 3-inch pot of soil, otherwise return the cutting to its first home and wait. Place the potted plants in bright (but not sunny) places where it's reasonably warm, and sit back and enjoy your free gift of nature.

Leaf Cuttings

You can clip leaves from many succulents and gesneriads and get new plants. Sounds incredible, but it works. Cut a leaf with a sterile razor blade, dip the severed end in rooting hormone, and insert it into the vermiculite or sand box (not in plain water as with cuttings). Leave half the leaf out and half in the medium. There are variations on the leaf-cutting business. Some plants, like sansevieria, can be multiplied by slicing a leaf in 2-inch sections. Insert the cut pieces one by one in rooting medium. Rex begonias are easily multiplied by simply making several cuts at the junction of veins in a leaf. Pin down the leaf in moist medium so the cut area is in contact with the medium; plants will appear at these junctions.

Offshoots

Look at the base of plants like agaves, orchids or bromeliads, and you'll see tiny replicas of the mother plant growing. Simply cut these off when they are about 3 inches high and pot them in soil to get new plants. Keep them somewhat warm and in a bright place to get them growing.

Division

This technical-sounding term merely means pulling a plant with crowns apart and taking each section and potting it separately to get new plants. To accomplish this trick, look down at a rosette-type plant such as a bromeliad or fern. You can almost see the divisions (clumps). Pull these apart gently with your hands, or cut them with a sharp knife, and pot them. Place them in a warm, bright place, and in a few weeks, growth will have started and you'll have a new plant. What an easy way to keep the larder well stocked!

Air Layering

Unlike the rest of the propagating methods, this one isn't easy. It's a complicated way of forcing a plant to grow roots midsection on a plant. Make a girdle or notch on the stem, cover the cut with sphagnum, wrap the cut, then spray. And pray.

Starting from Seed

This method is very satisfying, and I do suggest it to all, especially now when plants are becoming so expensive. You get a lot of seed for little money, and even though it does take time to get new plants, the wait is well worth the method. Furthermore, with so many seeds the odds are in your favor that you'll be successful. And besides, there's nothing as proud as a gardener with a plant he's started himself. It's his baby!

Use any container—same kinds as for cuttings—and sprinkle seeds on top of the growing medium. Imbed large seeds their girth; merely scatter small ones. Give good heat to the seeds (again, the top of the refrigerator works well), and keep them moist. If the seed medium gets dry or too wet, that's the end, so observe daily that the seed box is moist. Keep a Baggie on sticks over the unit, but never allow it to get too moist inside. When you see signs of new growth, add a very weak plant food solution once a week. When seedlings are 3 inches high they can be potted separately in small containers of soil.

Where to Buy Plants

Alberts & Merkel Bros., Inc.
   P.O. Box 537
   Boynton Beach, Fla.
   33435

Orchids,
   bromeliads, ferns

Burgess Seed & Plant Co.
   67 E. Battle Creek St.
   Galesburg, Mich. 49053

All kinds of
   house plants

W. Atlee Burpee Co.
   Philadelphia, Pa. 19132

All kinds of
   house plants

Fischer's Greenhouses
   Dept. HC
   Linwood, N.J. 08221

Gesneriads

Hauserman's Orchids
   Box 363
   Elmhurst, Ill. 60218

Orchids

Henrietta's Nursery
   1345 N. Brawley
   Fresno, Calif. 93705

Cacti and
   succulents

Margaret Ilgenfritz
   Box 665
   Monroe, Mich. 48161

Orchids

Johnson Cactus Gardens
   2735 Olive Hill Rd.
   Fallbrook, Calif. 92028

Cacti and
   succulents

Logee's Greenhouses
   55 North St.
   Danielson, Conn. 06239

House plants
   of all kinds

Merry Gardens
  Camden, Me. 04843

*House plants
of all kinds*

George W. Park Seed Co.
  Box 31
  Greenwood, S.C. 29646

House plants